47

June 29, 1974

Imogene + Troy Perry

Lovers of the Outer Banks.

Milford R. Ballance

THE HANDS OF TIME

THE
HANDS
OF TIME

MILFORD R. BALLANCE

VANTAGE PRESS

NEW YORK   WASHINGTON   HOLLYWOOD

FIRST EDITION

Published by Vantage Press, Inc.
516 West 34th Street, New York, N. Y. 10001

Manufactured in the United States of America

Standard Book No. 533-00183-8

PREFACE

North Carolina furnishes many historical incidents, a great number of legends, and a better understanding of our great pride, heritage, and culture. With the passing of time, there are many older people in the state who have watched a volume of mysteries. Many years ago, North Carolina began with an unsolved mystery—the Lost Colony, at Roanoke Island. Since then, many other events have taken place on this historical island; mysteries that were not recorded and seldom mentioned. It might well be called the "cradle of our nation."

For the first time in history, the true story of the *Hattie Creef* will be revealed in these pages. It has been necessary for me to dig deeply into the minds of the older natives in Dare County, especially on historical Roanoke Island, at Manteo and Wancheese, also in the village of Kitty Hawk, to get the hidden and almost forgotten true facts that have been buried in their minds for so many years about the *Hattie Creef*.

In order to have a better understanding, and a greater pride in our past of the hardships these people endured in this isolated portion of the earth along the Outer Banks of North Carolina, the astonishing true facts will be brought out into the open and made known to the readers of this book.

In the behavior of man and nature, many happenings that come and go are sometimes fascinating and also baffling. Much credit should be given to George Washington Creef Jr., for his bold and unusually stirring experience: A business venture to build the boat of his dreams, to move forward, and promote better transportation and communication for all mankind in this area.

CONTENTS

Chapter

THE HANDS OF TIME

CHAPTER ONE

Discoveries, Explorations, Disappointments, and Mysteries

In the following pages I shall endeavor to bring to the people of the world a better understanding of the hardships our fore-fathers encountered in order to establish a foothold on this great continent during the Age of Discovery.

Many of these adventurers possessed the quality and the duty of being loyal to their rulers and adhered to their leaders, while others chose the treacherous ways of piracy.

Very little was known about the world before the year of 1492. The people of Europe knew nothing of what lay far to the west of them across the vast Atlantic Ocean, just where they lived, and the land bordering the Mediterranean Sea. So many horrible stories about the great Atlantic Ocean left the people with wor-ried minds. They were taught to believe that terrible monsters would destroy any ship that dared sail upon it. A feeling of horror filled the minds of all adventurers.

By the year 1492, many changes had taken place. The compass, improved maps, and sailing charts were more accurate. The astrolabe had been invented, an instrument used by navigators to find the altitude of a star or a heavenly planet. It has now been replaced by the sextant.

The great Atlantic Ocean was still known to Europeans as the Sea of Darkness. But a new spirit arose in the people as the printing press was invented and many books were printed. The desire to explore and expand grew stronger because in the minds of some explorers soared the idea that the earth's surface had hardly been scratched.

As a boy Christopher Columbus lived in Genoa, Italy. He played and grew up around the docks, and eagerly listened to stories which the sailors told about the wonderful strange lands they had visited. It was here that he decided to become a good sailor and see those lands for himself.

Columbus' parents were poor; they could not afford to send him to school, but he borrowed and studied all the books he could get. The old-time sailors were always willing to answer his questions, and the mapmakers and other people who could tell him many useful and important things talked with him for hours. He listened, and remembered what they had told him.

When Columbus grew up, he went to live in Portugal, Spain. Here the people were well advanced in sailing. Prince Henry, a famous navigator, had built a school of navigation. Columbus did not believe that the world was flat; he argued that it was round. He wanted to find a better and shorter route to the East than going all the way around Africa.

Finally after several persuasive conversations with King Ferdinand and Queen Isabella, the rulers of Spain listened to him and agreed to provide him with three small ships—the *Pinta*, the *Niña*, and the *Santa Maria*.

In the summer of 1492, from Palos, Columbus sailed west on the Sea of Darkness. The European world had not known of any better courage and determination than that provided by the men who set sail in these tiny ships, which gradually disappeared on the horizon.

After seventy days and nights, riding out many violent strong winds and heavy seas, they crossed the broad and stormy Atlantic. The sky was clear, stars twinkled, heavenly bodies looked down with an epithet of approval on these weary but happy souls.

In the early morning hours on October 12, 1492, the *Pinta*, *Niña*, and the *Santa Maria*, flying the flag of the king of Spain, dropped anchor off the coast of an island in the Caribbean Sea. The decks of the small ships were crowded with men looking anxiously toward the shore. At last, Columbus thought, he had accomplished something. He was sure he had reached the rich spice islands of the East by sailing west.

At sunup Columbus and the captains of the other two ships went ashore and claimed the land for King Ferdinand of Spain, and named the island San Salvador. Then, with his men, he knelt and thanked God for their safe crossing of a terrifying and unknown sea.

Later this island turned out to be an island in the Bahamas, south of Florida, but it was here that the first discovery of

America was made. After short cruises among Haiti, Cuba, and other islands, Columbus returned to Spain.

Now France, England, and Holland wanted some of the riches in the New World, and soon men from these countries were exploring along the coast of America searching for gold. As time went by, some of these ships sailed into the mouth of the Cape Fear River and found rich land that is now North Carolina. The French explored the North Carolina coast in the spring of 1524. The Spanish made a visit to North Carolina in 1526. They too sailed up the Cape Fear River looking for a suitable place to settle. There were over five hundred men and women in the Spanish expedition. They brought with them Negro slaves and horses. The party was led by Lucas Vasquez de Ayllon. One of his ships was wrecked as it entered the mouth of the river. During the next few months he had a new ship constructed, the first ship to be built in North America by white men.

But everything seemed to go wrong for these settlers. Most of the Spanish settlers were taken sick with a fever and many of them died. The others moved south into what is now South Carolina. It was not long before more of the settlers also became ill and died, including Ayllon.

The survivors decided to go back to Santo Domingo. This was the end of the Spanish efforts to settle along the Carolina coast, so North Carolina was left to the Indians for many more years to come.

During the reign of Queen Elizabeth the First, many Englishmen thought it would be a good idea to begin a real colony in the New World. Sir Walter Raleigh was among the first to offer to spend his own money to plant the English colony in the New World. After talking frequently with the Queen, discussing his plans thoroughly in order to create a great interest, Elizabeth gladly gave her consent.

In the spring of 1584, Sir Walter Raleigh sent Philip Amadas and Arthur Barlowe, with two small ships well equipped with men and supplies, to find a good place to establish a colony. They sailed from England to the Canaries, and then westward along the same route that Columbus had followed. When they reached the West Indies, they drifted with the Gulf Stream. After sailing on for sixty-seven days they reached the North

Carolina coast, then sailed north for another hundred and twenty miles and entered the Pamlico Sound through Oregon Inlet. As soon as they landed they gave thanks to God for their safe voyage, and the land was claimed in the name of Queen Elizabeth.

A few days later, Barlowe and some of his men sailed twenty miles across Pamlico Sound. They came to an island which the Indians called Roanoke. One of the native chiefs made signs of joy and welcome, and received them cordially.

For several weeks they explored Roanoke Island and traded with the Indians. Tin dishes, copper kettles, trinkets, and other English articles were traded for animal skins. The settlers were greatly pleased with the attractive features of the coast.

They were amazed by the abundance of fruits, vegetables, and wild game. Delicious grapes were plentiful at Mother Vineyard near the north end of Roanoke Island, on the east side overlooking Roanoke Sound from the eight- to ten-foot sandbank along the shore. The surrounding waters in the sounds were filled with the best of seafood, such as fish, clams, and oysters, the best in all the world. Spreading oak trees grew in the rich soil, and were larger than those in England. Red cedars added to the beauty of this magnificent island. Surely Roanoke Island was the place to start a colony.

In mid-fall, Barlowe and Amadas decided to return to England. On Roanoke Island they had met two extremely friendly Indians who had helped them in many ways. Their names were Manteo and Wancheese. It was a long, slow journey back across the great Atlantic. Amadas was anxious to report his findings to Sir Walter Raleigh, and show the English people the kind of natives that lived in the New World.

When they arrived, Raleigh was delighted with the wonderful report. The English were greatly amazed when they saw the two Indians; Manteo and Wancheese were equally surprised when they got a glimpse of the white man's world in England. Queen Elizabeth was so pleased that she gave Raleigh many fine presents and also made him a knight. This is how he came to be called Sir Walter Raleigh.

Now the English people began to make plans to claim all the land that now extends from Florida to Canada. The Queen was not married and was called the Virgin Queen, so they named these lands in the New World "Virginia" in honor of Queen Elizabeth.

Very little time was lost before Raleigh sent out another colony to Virginia. This time a fleet of seven ships, well supplied and manned, was on its way. The Queen gave him one of the seven ships, and Secretary of State Francis Walsingham, and others, helped to finance the expedition.

Under the command of Sir Richard Grenville the fleet sailed from Plymouth in April 1585. The men were to get the land ready to build homes for their families. In the group were Governor Ralph Lane; the artist John White, who went with them to draw maps and pictures of the wonderful sights in the New World; Amadas and the Indians Manteo and Wancheese; and there were also a preacher and a physician with them.

After three long exciting months on the ocean, the ships reached the North Carolina coast. A strong east wind and high seas prevented them from entering any of the inlets along the dangerous coast for the next five days. Then all of a sudden the wind lulled, the sea calmed, and the thick heavy mist disappeared in brilliant sunshine.

At noon on April 25, they sailed into Oregon Inlet and into the Pamlico Sound. Here the seven ships dropped anchor until the following morning. Day broke dark and gloomy; dense fog provided a shroud for the area, brought in from the ocean across the narrow strip of land by a steady southeast wind. By the middle of the morning the fog was gone, sails were hoisted in position, and the small ships slowly moved ahead. The afternoon sun blazed a brilliant trail on the surface of the water as they sailed across Pamlico Sound. Just before nightfall they reached the shores of Roanoke Island.

Early the next day, the men immediately began to build a fort on the island for protection against unfriendly or hostile Indians. After the fort was finished, they named it Fort Raleigh. They also built houses inside the fort. This settlement was the first English colony in America. The men in the colony were very happy over the prospects of this successful adventure.

On September 3, Governor Lane wrote a letter to Richard Hakluyt in London. It was the first letter ever sent from an English colony in the New World. He wrote about the rich soil, fruit trees, beautiful forests, wild game, and delicious wild grapes. He also stated that England might get flax, drugs, and many other valuable things from this land of plenty.

But the island was not so rich in wealth as Governor Lane had described it. Instead of planting crops, the colonists spent their time exploring and searching for gold. Some even looked for a northwest passage to the Pacific Ocean. Although Chief Manteo had helped them from the start, they still had problems. They needed better leadership and more supplies; and the wild behavior of savage Indian tribes was a great threat to their survival. They continued to live in suspense.

The geography point of view was not good. The dangerous coast, the lack of a good inlet nearby, and the shallow water of the surrounding sounds made it far from a good place to develop outside trade. When winter came their food supply was low, clothes were scarce, ammunition was almost gone; all this meant a rough winter ahead. In a few days, Grenville agreed to return to England for more supplies.

Manteo still remained friendly and helped them; but Wancheese and other Indians began to hate the settlers, and soon were busy making plans to destroy the colony. When Governor Lane learned about their plans, he and his men attacked the Indians and killed many of them.

This made things worse, for now the colony was in great danger. Sir Francis Drake, with his fleet of ships not far from the coast, and not far from Roanoke Island, offered to take the hungry settlers back to England. They gladly accepted.

This ended the first English Colony in America on Roanoke Island after about ten months of hardships. Later, when Grenville finally returned to Roanoke Island with supplies, he was too late. But he left a few of his men to claim the land for England.

The first settlers found no gold, but they did find tobacco, corn, and potatoes. The colony had failed, but it had been

16

the first English colony in the New World. They also had about seventy-five beautiful famous paintings of Indian life by John White.

Sir Walter Raleigh was very sad and disappointed with the failure of his first colony because he had lost most of his fortune in the adventure. This, however, did not stop him; he refused to give up. He received help mostly from English merchants to help pay expenses of his second colony. He was sure that this time things would be different. He again sent John White, the artist who had been with the first expedition and who had drawn the maps and the pictures of the Indians. This time White would be the Governor. No more servants would be sent but rather landowners, and five-hundred acres was to be allotted to each colonist.

Raleigh also sent their wives and children so they could have real homes away from home. In all, one hundred and seventeen sailed from England on three ships in May 1587. One of the men in the group was Governor White's son-in-law, Ananias Dare. One of the seventeen women was Ananias' wife Eleanor, daughter of Governor White.

Because large ships could not get close to Roanoke Island, Sir Walter Raleigh instructed Governor White to pick up the men Grenville had left at Roanoke Island, sail on up the coast to Chesapeake Bay and then make their settlement there where the water was deeper and better suited for trade. Also, the Indians were more friendly than those at Roanoke Island.

When Governor White reached Roanoke Island in July, the Captain of the fleet, Fernandez, refused to take them any further. When they went ashore, they found Fort Raleigh in ruins. There was no sign of the men left by Grenville the year before, but only skeletons lying about on the ground among the tall weeds that waved in the light breeze.

Governor White's men began to rebuild the fort, and after many days of hard work it was finished. Homes were built inside the fort for their families to live in just as before. They agreed to name the fort The City of Raleigh in Virginia. On Sunday, August 13, they held the first Protestant religious meeting (or service) in the New World.

It was here that the faithful Indian Manteo was baptized and

17

given the title Lord of Roanoke, the first title an American Indian had ever held.

On Friday, August 18, 1587, Eleanor Dare gave birth to a baby girl. The parents were very happy. This was the first white child to be born in America of English parents, the first to be born in the New World. She was baptized and named Virginia Dare.

Supplies were getting low and would not last the colony through the coming winter. Governor White was asked to return to England and get the things they needed. His granddaughter, Virginia Dare, was only nine days old when he once again set sail for England.

The day before he sailed, the settlers promised Governor White that if they left Roanoke Island before he returned they would carve on a tree, or on the fort, the name or place of their new home. If they were in trouble, they would carve a cross above the name.

After another long and dangerous voyage across the Atlantic, Governor White reached England. He found his country at war with Spain. This meant no return to Roanoke Island until the war was over, because no ships were allowed to leave English ports.

Finally after three years, Governor White was given permission to return to his colony. As the ship approached Roanoke Island, its guns roared out a thundering signal. But there was no answer. The next day the men went ashore. As they drew closer, they saw carved on a tree the letters CRO. Someone had left the message unfinished. Where to now? The men rushed on to the City of Raleigh, but found the fort vacant and lying in ruins. The houseroofs had fallen in and the whole fort was overgrown with weeds, bushes, and thick grass. Small pieces of broken armor lay scattered on the ground, and not a living person was in sight. On a post of the unoccupied ghostly fort was the word CROATAN, but no cross was carved over it.

Silence was broken as Governor White and his men knelt to pray. Maybe the people were safe with the Indians that lived only a few miles away on the sandbanks at Croatan. Some of the men tried hard to get to Croatan, but a broken cable on the ship, along with other troubles prevented them from going.

Governor White's heart grew heavy as many things began to

move rapidly through his mind. He never found little Virginia Dare or any of the colonists he had left behind three years previously. Several searches were made in later years, but the "Lost Colony" was never found.

At this time there were more than thirty thousand Indians in North Carolina. Their fierce, primitive ways were unbelievable. The hatred these savage Indians held in their hearts for this small peaceful colony was pure savagery. Manteo talked with the chiefs of the other tribes, but he received only contemptuous treatment.

It was a blessing that at least Manteo was a friend of the colonists. He was a very powerful and skilled warrior in North Carolina. There were twenty-nine tribes, each with a different name. Some were friendly; but most of them loved to fight, kill, burn villages, capture the young maidens and squaws and carry them away and use them to increase and strengthen their tribes. The Hatteras tribe lived on Roanoke Island. Although Manteo could not do very much alone with his people, chiefs of other tribes feared and respected him. In this way he was able to delay their desires.

From what we have been able to put together, ask yourselves what really did happen to the Lost Colony? Did they die as a result of some sort of fever or plague? Were they killed by the Indians? Did they try to return to their homeland, but were swallowed up by the sea? Did they actually go to Croatan? Were they forced by hardships to join some Indian tribe in order to survive?

Today there are four large sounds surrounding Roanoke Island; but in those days, on the west side of the island there was no sound but only small narrow streams. You could lay a ten-foot rail or log down and walk across the marsh through the scraggy windblown trees and bushes. Wild cranberries grew there by the acre.

Governor White could have walked about three miles west to Croatan. Why didn't he, or some of his men go? To this day no one has found the answer. Now where the dark-red delicious cranberries once grew, there is a large sound about three and a half miles wide. It separates Roanoke Island from Manns Harbor. (The name has been changed from Croatan in the early days, to Manns Harbor.)

High winds and waves during Outer Banks storms had washed this low land away over a period of time, and nature formed a beautiful natural navigable waterway—the Croatan Sound. This sound is not only profitable to the fishermen and convenient for transportation but also has increased the value and beauty of this famous historical island as it unceasingly washes its shores.

The hands of time moved on. Now Sir Walter Raleigh did not have enough money to send out another colony, but he still did not lose faith in settling or establishing a successful group of people in this distant land. He wrote: "I shall yet live to see in this New World an English nation."

In 1606, London merchants received permission from King James of England to again try to plant colonies in the New World. Some of the men who had helped Raleigh to plant his second colony began to make plans.

With treacherous sandbars, such as Diamond Shoals along the North Carolina coast, the dangerous inlets, shallow rivers and sounds, along with the costly experience learned from the failure of Sir Walter Raleigh's two previous colonies was reason enough to be more cautious.

After riding out many storms and long lonely days and dark nights, the tiny ships approached the North Carolina coast but did not attempt to enter any of its inlets. Instead they sailed north for about fifty miles. Here they found surpassing entrance through the Chesapeake Bay from the sea to deep harbors, with maximum protection from high winds and raging seas.

Having to depend on trade with the European countries, mainly England, until they could become established, made it more understandable why they needed good natural harbors.

Although the settlers had a hard time for many years that followed, the first permanent English colony in America was established at Jamestown, Virginia, in 1607.

North Carolina had been left to the Indians for about seventy years after Sir Walter Raleigh's colony was lost on Roanoke Island, before white people came here to stay. Most of them came by land from the colony in Virginia. For this reason it was about fifty-four years later before there were any towns in

North Carolina. It was strictly Indian country until about the year 1660.

Anyone might safely say that North Carolina had practically everything that the early settlers needed, except good natural harbors for trade and navigation even though it has a very long coast line for a distance of three hundred and twenty miles.

Here, along the Outer Banks, there is a long chain of islands, with Ocracoke being the largest. Some of these islands and sandbanks are only a few feet high, while others at Kill Devil Hill in Dare County are over a hundred feet high. Only a short distance away, to the south of these bleak sand hills at Nags Head, you will find Jockeys' Ridge, which is the highest and largest coastal sand dune along the Atlantic Coast.

Between this long strip of sandy beaches and the mainland there are several sounds—the Pamlico, Albemarle, Currituck, Roanoke, Croatan, Core, and Bogue.

The inlets from the Atlantic Ocean, through the banks and into the sounds, are shallow and shifted by the terrific force of the high waves and strong currents during northeast storms and hurricanes. This made it very dangerous in the early days for ships to enter. Most of the sounds are shallow; only small ships, sailed by skillful sailors, could find their way safely through these inlets.

So anyone can understand why the early settlers, after the most fertile land along the James River was taken, moved farther south by land instead of by water.

In 1650, many settlers moved into what is now known as the Albemarle section of North Carolina and built homes along the Chowan River. Some of these settlers came to North Carolina because they wanted more fredom than they had under the rule of the Jamestown Governor White. Others explored for riches in gold, silver, and precious stone; but, to their disappointment, they found no gold at this time.

As the hands of time moved on, people came from Germany, Scotland, England, Ireland, France, Spain, Switzerland, and many other countries to settle in this wonderful state of North Carolina. They too were afraid of the dangerous shoals and inlets along the coast, and came into this country by the blessing of this deep natural harbor from the sea through the Chesapeake Bay where they could land more safely.

A short while later people from foreign lands came overland in covered wagons; some came on horseback, some on foot, all were seeking their fortune.

Another threat to these brave early settlers that could not be forgotten was that twenty-nine unfriendly tribes of Indians roamed practically every section of North Carolina. Imagine thirty or thirty-five thousand wild, fierce Indians wandering about the wilderness searching for human scalps! Many hostile savage tribes lived in the coastal area. The Hatteras tribe, with whom the first white settlers had contact, lived on Roanoke Island.

Also the most merciless pirates in the world murdered and robbed along the coast of North Carolina. Deep rivers and smooth waters in the sounds near Ocracoke Inlet made good hiding places for pirate ships. What is now known as Silver Lake, where the village of Ocracoke is built on the Outer Banks, has a narrow channel which connects the beautiful lake with Pamlico Sound.

Here Edward Teach, better known as "Blackbeard" because of his thick black beard, kept his ships hidden. Blackbeard was the most dangerous pirate along the coast. His fleet of ships was small enough to enter through the inlets and find shelter in the sounds, while his men watched from the tops of trees for ships that passed by or came near the coast. Each pirate ship was armed with a cannon.

Blackbeard's men were a band of criminals wanted in all parts of the world for robberies, rape, and many other crimes. They made their living by robbing merchant ships, and murdered anyone who tried to stop them.

When approaching their prey they fired their cannons at the ship, killed the crew, and took all the cargo on board. Sometimes they kept the ship they captured; at other times they destroyed it. The loot they carried to their hiding places where it was kept until sold. Some of the merchant ships, in those days, carried gold and silver. When a chest of gold was taken, Blackbeard carried it ashore and buried it on one of the islands.

Finally the people of North Carolina complained to Governor Eden, but he refused to do anything about it. The people became very angry, and some of the settlers asked the Governor in Virginia to help them. Soon Captain Robert Maynard and two British ships were sent to hunt for the pirates.

Captain Maynard found Blackbeard's ships near Ocracoke Inlet, about one mile offshore. The pirates watched as the British ships came nearer. The sea was calm, warmth from the blazing sun overhead was felt, and tension mounted as they began to close in facing each other.

Suddenly the pirates fired all their cannons. Many of Captain Maynard's men were killed. He sent his men below deck, leaving the dead and wounded behind. Blackbeard's ship sailed in close to Maynard's. Quickly he and his men rushed aboard. As Blackbeard and his men reached the deck, Captain Maynard and his crew came up from below with guns and swords drawn.

During the hand-to-hand battle that followed, Captain Maynard killed Blackbeard by stabbing him in the throat. The rest of the pirates surrendered.

By 1665, many people in North Carolina were living on farms throughout the region north of the Albemarle Sound. This region included what is now Currituck County and helped to begin the history of North Carolina as the home of the English people, English customs, and the English language.

One of the most important factors in the state of North Carolina history down through the years has been its climate and location. It is located between latitudes 33° 27′ 37″ and 36° 34′ 25″. Also meridians of longitudes 75° 27′, and 84° 20′. This means that the state lies entirely within the warm part of the temperate zone. Early settlers liked the region near the coast because the climate was mild. They were pleased with the long growing season and the plentiful rainfall.

In 1709, more explorers and settlers found a great variety of plants and vegetables being grown by the Indians—corn, peas, tobacco, beans, potatoes, squash, and pumpkins. Fruits and berries grew wild. Almost everywhere there were strawberries, large and sweet. Apples, peaches, plums, and figs were delicious and also growing wild in the forest. Blackberries, huckleberries, dewberries, and raspberries were plentiful. Grapes in great quantities were also found.

Rivers and sounds were alive with the best eating fish in the whole world, as well as oysters, clams, and shrimp. The forests were full of wild animals—rabbits, squirrels, wild turkeys, deer, wild boar, black bear, and many others roamed quietly from place to place through the dense and tall whispering virgin pine. Quail, robins, blackbirds, doves, wild ducks and geese provided food in season, all of which added to the great natural advantages of these early settlers of eastern North Carolina. This was truly a great part of the country with God's blessings.

At this early age eastern North Carolina had many huge forests studded with longleaf pine, red oak, white oak, live oak, gum, cypress, juniper, and cedar. But as the population grew and spread throughout the state, more and more land was cleared for raising crops. Trees were destroyed by fires, and much valuable timber was cut down to make room for farmlands and to build more homes.

As the years slowly passed, over three hundred different kinds of minerals were found in the State of North Carolina. In 1799 gold was found in the Piedmont section near what is now Concord. Between 1799 and 1860, more than $50 million worth of gold was mined in the state, so that it was called the "Golden State."

Until 1870, all the Outer Banks, including Roanoke Island and Hatteras, were in Currituck County territory because Dare County had not been formed. At Nags Head, in the early 1830s, only a few scattered small crude houses dotted the woods of the early settlers. Kitty Hawk also was a part of Currituck County. Some of the homes were built of lumber and shingles salvaged from wrecked ships that drifted ashore on the beaches along the North Carolina coast during storms which produced high winds and wild mountainous waves.

Residents from the mainland especially like Nags Head as a summer vacationing resort but only some of the wealthier class could afford to go. A few vacationing families from Elizabeth City, in Pasquotank County, in Edenton, of Chowan, and a few Bertie County planters, along with a few from Perquimans County liked to roam the beaches during the summer months. Many of them would climb to the top of Jockey Ridge, which is the tallest and largest sand hill along the coast, and watch the ships pass by with their cargo.

The sealanes offshore from the Outer Banks were in continual use in 1837. Ships came from all main ports of the world. Some carried raw materials, coffee, sugar, coconuts, molasses, and lumber; others brought coal, passengers, and mail.

During this period the ships were of many shapes and sizes, mostly sailing vessels of different types, ranging from full-rigged packets to barks and extravagant, overdecorated, irregularly shaped baroque style boats from many foreign ports. Naval ships could be seen as they continually patrolled the coastline offshore.

Many happy hours were leisurely passed by the summer colony watching these strange schooners sail back and forth, splitting the waters of the rolling blue Atlantic. On clear days, from the top of the highest sand dune along the Atlantic Coast, people walking on the decks of ships could be seen with the naked eye, while gentle cool breezes blew in from the ocean across sand hot from the summer sun. Young lovers sat and watched fleecy white, uneven, cumulus clouds resting leisurely at ease along the horizon, seemingly on the vast ocean's surface, while whitecaps, formed by the wind and force of the water breaking against the sandbars, rode the unceasing waves to the shore and washed high up on the pebble-studded sandy beach and then disappeared in the form of mist. Their thoughts searched the lonely waters while the summer sun blazed down and bathed them in a sea of love.

People from the mainland were amazed and greatly impressed by the primitive ways and the unusual traditions that were still practiced by the natives, due mostly to being isolated from other parts of the state because of poor transportation and communication.

Wild ponies wandered about in herds along the Outer Banks, feeding on coarse salt grass, sea oats, evergreen bushes, and marsh sage. Strong savage stallions watched over their flocks. Each stallion ruled his own group of affectionate colorful mares. To obtain fresh drinking water, nature had taught them to paw a hole in the sand, deep enough to reach water. According to legend, their ancestors, one of the finest breeds of horses in the world, came from Arabia.

Many years ago, a cargo of Arabian horses was being shipped to America for breeding purposes. When the sailing vessel ran into a northeast storm off the North Carolina coast and was forced ashore by mountainous waves and strong winds, and the schooner began to break up and go to pieces from the tremendous pounding of the heavy seas, some of these Arabian horses swam a few hundred feet to the beach and survived.

These ponies were usually small, due to the lack of proper food, although some were of normal size and possessed the qualities of a fine breed. As time passed, many natives began claiming separate herds. Once each year they held a horse-penning and the colts were marked by their owners with a branding iron. Some of the older ponies were rounded up, loaded on a flat-bottom barge, and pulled across the Currituck Sound to the mainland where they were auctioned off to the highest bidder.

CHAPTER TWO

Birthplace of George Washington Creef, Jr.

About twelve miles west of Roanoke Island, across the Croatan Sound and past Manns Harbor, on the mainland not far from the water's edge there was a small village called East Lake. Here lived George and Rebecca Creef with their children.

On September 11, 1856, a son was born to them. They named him George Washington Creef, Jr., after his father. Rebecca's husband, during his childhood, had been nicknamed "Wash" for short.

Wash Creef now stood by the bedside of his lovely wife and looked down at his infant son. Wash was very happy.

It was late in the afternoon. He turned and walked a few steps across the dim unpainted room to an open window. A burning heat was felt from the September sun as it slanted in through the small opening. He gazed down at the long dark shadows on the ground of the leaning moss-covered barn and shelter, and watched as the faithful black-and-white milk cow came hurriedly down the lane that led to the barn from the spreading live oak grove of dark-green trees.

Then the sound of pounding hoofs filled the air and a pale bay horse stopped in front of the barn door. Puffs of dust marked the trail he had taken from the field. He snorted and bent his head as he moved closer to nibble at the ends of the corn shucks, which hung from the cracks in the sagging, worn, partly closed barn door. Chickens, turkeys, and other fowl gathered around.

The bay was different from the droves of wild, shaggy, poorly fed ponies that roamed the isolated woods and beaches along the Outer Banks. When he was just a small colt he had wandered away from a drove of wild ponies and had been captured while swimming a wide creek.

Wash and Rebecca were fishing when they spotted the bay trying to swim across the creek. After quite a bit of scuffling the bay was safely brought home, along with a bushel-basket filled with spots and jumping mullets which would be salted down in a wooden keg for the winter days that were soon to come.

They named the bay Nag. After being well fed he grew into a sleek, tame, clean-limbed animal that added striking beauty to the farmyard.

It was now feeding time. The restless fowl and animals gathered nearer the barn door. Wash slowly turned and left the window. Stopping beside the bed, he gave his wife a kiss on her cheek, while an understanding smile covered her face. Then he walked down to the first floor and on to the kitchen.

Unfortunately for the natives at East Lake, there were no doctors in this part of the world. During childbirth, a so-called "Granny woman" took the place of a doctor and served as midwife. She would also help out with the cooking and household chores for about a week, or as long as she was needed. In this case, there was Miss Nancy. She was well experienced, understanding, and a lovable aging woman.

A pot of coffee steamed on the wood-burning kitchen stove. The aroma of browning clabber biscuits inside the iron oven filled the room. Large, lean, hickory smoked slices of home-cured ham frying in the cast-iron "spider" caused Wash to slow his pace as he entered the kitchen. When he turned to pick up a glowing ember of tobacco that had fallen to the floor from his pipe, the bright blaze from the burning wood in the stove shone on his tired sun-browned face. He strolled on through the room to the back porch, then a short distance across the yard toward the barn where his livestock restlessly pranced back and forth waiting to be fed, watered, and secured for the night.

But as Wash strolled across the backyard on his way to the barn, his pace began to slow. Already he was thinking about the future of his newborn son, George Washington Creef, Jr. Many thoughts ran through his weary mind as he stopped beneath the huge, spreading oak tree that stood only a few feet away from the corner of the house. This giant oak had seen many generations come and go.

Leaning slightly backward and looking up through the large branches as if to find an answer to his mixed-up solitary thoughts, he did not hear the rustling noise of the thick colorful leaves on the little stems as the wind moved them hurriedly in every direction.

Wash turned toward the barn moving with caution through the noisy feathered fowl that ran back and forth across his feet near the barn door. Nag began to nudge his nose against his arm as he reached to remove the worn wood peg that kept the barn door from opening. Corn was shucked, shelled and scattered on the ground in front of the barn for the fowl. Nag stood in the stable with his nose in the manger biting the corn off the cob, crushing and grinding it up with his teeth. Beside him in the next stall the old milk cow slowly chewed and ate her portion of nubbins along with the hay. The barn door closed and the peg was put into place. The feeding chores were finished, another day was ending. Slowly Wash walked toward the house stopping once again beneath the oak where his thoughts returned to wander.

What did he have to offer his son? Would his boy have to drift with the tide of time, as he himself had practically had to do? Or would he be able to venture out beyond this isolated lonely part of the world, away from the unrest and strife to which the natives had become so accustomed and had to bear, with little or no change, since the days of the early settlers?

Just then Miss Nancy opened the oven door and set the round tin pan of hot biscuits on the door in front of the oven so they would keep warm. Then she placed a dish of meat on the table beside a thick, yellow stone bowl of hot brown gravy. Gray steam escaped slowly from the spout of the coffeepot which rested on the back of the stove.

Supper was ready.

Miss Nancy wondered what was keeping Wash with his livestock so long. With caution she approached the door that opened out on the porch, and saw him standing beneath the oak tree. To her, he appeared to be in deep meditation.

The sound of her footsteps on the porch, and the calling of a crow as it flew low overhead on his way to roost, suddenly returned Wash Creef's mind back to present surroundings. While he turned and slowly moved toward the kitchen, his thoughts deadened and gradually drifted away.

Stopping at the steps to the porch to beat the excess dust from his pants cuffs and shoes, he noticed that Miss Nancy was watching the setting sun. It was like a huge red ball of fire, and hung just above the dark and silent cedar trees that stood strikingly against the bright blaze of the sun.

Late afternoon shadows lengthened as they crept over the yard. Wash showed every sign of being tired as he climbed up the steps and walked across the worn boards to the far end of the narrow, gloomy, closed-in end of the porch. Here stood an old wooden bucket on a low bench fastened to the wall. Water drawn from the well a few minutes before clung to its sides, reflecting on its still surface the glow from the lamp which burned in the kitchen.

The dipper, made from a brown and fuzzy coconut shell, now worn slick and its color changed to a grayish black, was still being used by the family.

Some years ago a sailing schooner, loaded with coconuts, had run aground on one of the many dangerous shoals along the coast of the Outer Banks. After it broke into splinters from the pounding of the merciless monstrous waves during a sudden storm that came out of the northeast, coconuts were strewn for miles along the surf. The natives had made many useful and decorative items from the shells, such as candle holders, ashtrays, birdhouses, and water dippers.

Quietly removing the day's dirt from his face and hands with homemade soap, which his wife had made from animal fat and skins in the iron pot that rested on three legs in the corner of the kitchen, Wash gazed at the washbowl on the bench as he dried his hands. The bowl was made from a block of ash wood. By using an adz and a drawing knife he had been able to hollow it out and shape it into a useful washbasin. Before using it, hot mullet-fat oil was allowed to soak deeply into the wood and dry thoroughly to make it waterproof. This treatment also made the bowl last for many years.

Supper waited. Wash strolled toward the kitchen door. Once again he noticed the beauty and loveliness of the day as it came to an end. He was a great admirer of nature. Now the sun disappeared behind the trees, and twilight was fading away. The path that wound past the back gate led to the small patch of corn, now cut and standing in tall round shocks that began to loom in the distance like little Indian wigwams.

Nightfall once more hovered and then descended on this scattered little hamlet. Lamps had been filled with oil, wicks trimmed, and the globes or chimneys were sparkling clean. Wash stepped inside the kitchen, walked across the room, and sat down at one end of the table in the corner of the kitchen, away from the stove, and began to eat.

The silently burning oil lamps gave light to the rooms that were being used. Miss Nancy was busy rocking and humming to little George by the bedside, while Rebecca enjoyed her meal. Never had any family ever been drawn closer together than the Creef family tonight.

Soon all were gathered in the bedroom, discussing the events of the day, while the children listened and eagerly watched their little brother smile as he slept on the pillow beside his mother.

Memories of the past now held their interest. Smoke curled and drifted slowly from Wash's corn-cob pipe as he sat and puffed near the window. Many events were discussed, especially the storms, shipwrecks, and the dangerous shoals along the coast of the Outer Banks of North Carolina, all of which provided excitement and surprises—the unsolved mystery of the Lost Colony on Roanoke Island, only about twelve miles away; the strange hoof marks at Bath in North Carolina; and many other topics entered into their conversation.

The tick-tock, tick-tock of the old mantle clock in the living room below grew with great intensity as the informal exchange of ideas began to fade away. It was eleven-thirty. Light from the oil-burning lamp blazed up brightly as Miss Nancy turned the screw that raised the wick a bit to see more clearly while she prepared to tuck in Rebecca and her infant son safely for the night.

It had been an exciting, thrilling day for Miss Nancy and the Creef family. Silence now filled the room. Outside the wind blew from the east, making a soft rustling noise as it whispered through the large oak leaves while they slept. Miss Nancy rose early the next morning and cooked breakfast for the family and for herself, while Wash was busy feeding and looking after his stock. On the way from the corncrib to the kitchen, the aroma of salt mullets frying in the pan on the wood stove and mingling with the savor from the perking coffee was very stimulating to his early morning appetite.

Nag munched on his corn while the family ate breakfast. Then Wash climbed the stairs to see Rebecca and little George before leaving for the day. Nag was watered at the trough, which had been hollowed from a log by hand with an adz. Green moss covered the crude trough. The water was cool and fresh.

East Lake, the water which gave verdure to the growing trees, bushes, and grass along its shores, added beauty to this lonely village. With its various kinds of fish and wild fowl, it also helped to make living possible in this isolated part of North Carolina.

Little was seen of Wash during the day. He was kept busy hauling newmown hay, which had been cured by the warm September sun, and storing it in the barn loft before unfavorable weather drew near. Nag chewed on a mouthful of ripe hay while his master piled it higher and higher on the cart to which Nag was hitched. Wash stopped long enough to remove his frazzled straw hat and with his sleeve wipe the sweat from his brow.

He gazed with tired eyes down the wide green slope toward the lake, then climbed up on the high load of hay and started for home. To this land he owed his life. Wash was worn and aging. He felt that he could not escape being involved in whatever plight might befall this modest tiny neighborhood at East Lake.

Nag quickly swung the load of hay around and walked toward the pine grove by the side of the field. Dust rose and disappeared behind them as they moved down the winding path that led to the back gate of the barnyard. This was the last load of hay. Wash would be finished just before nightfall.

Afternoon sun had flooded the field with golden glory, while coveys of quail flew swiftly about. Heavy sounds made by Nag's hoofs thumped loudly as he crossed the log bridge near the gate. He was breathing hard from the strain of hauling the heavy load as he slowly approached the open door of the hay loft. In a short time Nag was free, roaming among the noisy fowl in the barnyard, and nibbling tender green grass that grew in clusters in the fence-locks.

Rebecca was watching from the upstairs window as Wash drew bucket after bucket full of clear, cool water from the deep stone

32

well and filled the moss-covered trough beneath the oak tree. A smile crossed her face as he walked up the steps that led to the back porch and the kitchen, a path he had trod so many times before.

For her, it had been a long and tedious warm day. But for Wash it had passed rather quickly because he had been hurrying to finish harvesting and storing his hay.

Miss Nancy opened the door and gave Wash a clean towel as he passed her on his way to the washbasin.

A large bowl of greens, meat, and potatoes, which had been prepared for supper, scented the room. Wash was tired and felt exhausted as he slowly climbed the stairs to see his wife and little George before supper. He was breathing deeply as he entered the room. Little George had been asleep most of the day, but now his big blue eyes were rather tense—as if he was busy looking with amazement at these strange kinfolks.

Miss Nancy came up with Rebecca's supper, and sent Wash and the other children down to the kitchen. Rebecca enjoyed the large platter of collards, potatoes, hogshead, hot biscuits, and a tall glass of fresh milk. Soon the meal was finished, and they all sat by the window and witnessed another beautiful sunset.

Oil lamps that were so carefully cleaned, filled with oil, wicks trimmed, now were standing ready to be lit. Twilight was slowly fading away as they all gathered together once more in the bedroom where Rebecca waited to hear about the activities of the day.

The conversation nearly always gradually found its way back to the many unsolved mysteries of the past. The legends, historical events, and other baffling secrets of the ocean that washes our North Carolina coast along the Outer Banks, are very fascinating.

After Wash finished his talk about the abundance of the hay he had stored in the loft of the sagging old barn, a moment of silence ensued during which no one voiced his thoughts. Wash sat against the wall, smoking his pipe. The soft yellow light from the wick in the lamp chimney burned steady and reflected on his tired, suntanned, lean face as he ran his fingers through his gray thinning hair and ruffled it.

Rebecca suddenly returned to the family chat by mentioning

the mysterious vanishing of Theodosia Burr along the treacherous stretch of dreaded coastline of the Hatteras and Nags Head section of the Outer Banks. Theodosia was the daughter of Aaron Burr, who once was the Vice-President of the United States and respected as a great statesman. Her charm, the quality of her behavior, calm self-possession and self-respect led to the honor that had been bestowed on her in society by all and had won for her the heart of Joseph Alston.

Aaron Burr, and Alexander Hamilton, who had been Secretary of the Treasury of the United States, often disagreed on political as well as on personal matters. Finally Burr challenged Hamilton to a pistol duel, which sometimes was the tradition in the early days.

After Burr killed Hamilton, it seems he had plotted with someone to establish a colony in the territory somewhere west of the Mississippi River. This was said to have been done in preparation for a war with Spain. Burr was charged with treason, and the Republican Party cast him aside. Later he was tried in the high court for treason at Richmond, Virginia, but was acquitted. He spent the next few years in Europe, living the life of a poor friendless hermit in great need.

His beautiful daughter became the wife of Governor Joseph Alston of South Carolina, one of that state's early governors. Theodosia married at the age of eighteen. In all of her father's misfortunes, she came to his rescue and helped him in every way possible.

From reliable sources Theodosia heard about her father living far away in poverty. This grieved her very much. With the help of her husband, Burr's return to the United States was made possible in 1812. Many people, both rich and poor, admired her devotion to her father in the dark days of his exile and disgrace.

Theodosia knew that her father was very unpopular at this time, so she made arrangements to sail on a small pilot boat, the *Patriot*, from Georgetown, South Carolina. She was to sail along the Atlantic coast to New York, and meet her father there.

On December 29, 1812, the *Patriot* set sail, taking on board the beautiful and admired by all people Theodosia Burr Alston, her maid, her baggage, including a portrait of herself, and, of course, the Captain and his crew.

At this time there was trouble between the United States and England. Part of the English fleet was lingering close to the Atlantic Coast somewhere in the area of Nags Head. Governor Alston had written a letter and given it to his wife to be presented to the Admiral of the British fleet, asking for safe passage to New York if the *Patriot* actually was stopped by any of the fleet.

Many other risky and tangible dangers also imperiled their voyage, besides the enemy fleet, such as pirates, storms, and the many hidden shoals along the coast of the Outer Banks.

On January 5, the *Patriot* actually did run afoul of the British fleet not many miles off Cape Hatteras. But according to legend, she was granted her passage after the Governor's request had been read.

As fate would have it, that same night a storm with hurricane force struck the North Carolina coast in the same area. From then on, so far as could be verified from reliable sources and records, neither the *Patriot* nor anyone aboard was ever seen again.

The clock on the hand-carved mantle in the living room began delivering an impressive sound—eight, nine, ten, eleven chimes. Everyone squirmed, moving a little from the motionless calm position each had assumed while Rebecca spoke about the mystery slowly looking about with questioning eyes, and wondering what actually did happen to the lovely Theodosia Burr Alston. Moments later all were snug in their beds, fast asleep.

Harvest time was in full bloom. The following week Wash was very busy repairing the customary proper location near the worn juniper rail-fence to store the following twelve months' supply of sweet potatoes. This old storage house was directly back of the barn at the edge of the field, near a large, dark-green, collard patch. It was narrow and long, rather gawky looking, with an oval shoulder-high sharp roof. A low door, just large enough for a person to crawl inside, swung leisurely with the southwest wind. The frame part was made of wood and covered with about two feet of light-brown dry pine straw, and soil about fifteen inches thick was placed on the straw to form the outside part of the potato house. Fresh dry and smooth straw from the dense thicket nearby covered the floor twenty-four inches thick inside where the potatoes were carefully poured and stored for the winter.

During extremely bitter cold weather, a lighted oil lantern hung inside to prevent freezing. After covering the potatoes with another thick layer of straw, the door was closed and fastened.

Nearby beside the garden stood a large drooping pear tree. Bushels of Bartlett pears firmly held onto its hanging, heavy-laden branches. Large orange pumpkins, made more visible as the big leaves on the vine turned yellow, bowed their heads from the brisk, light, frosty night air.

CHAPTER THREE

Unforgettable Footsteps

Miss Nancy was back home in her quiet lonely little three-room, run-down haven where she had lived all alone for many years. After staying with the Creef family for almost two weeks, and having such a delightful time, she could hardly bear the loneliness. Her imagination was running wild; everything seemed so different and so motionless.

The voices of night haunted her thoughts. She stood by the partly open sagging door, looking out across the yard. Dark-green friendly cedars now appeared so weird, like witches or great demons chained to earth, as she peered out through the pale-gray gloom of nightfall. Never had she felt this way before during her lonely last fifteen years since her dear old mother had been laid to rest just outside the yard a few feet away from the corner of the shabby little shack.

Slowly Miss Nancy stepped inside and closed the creepy creaking door. The oil lamp was lit and shining brightly against the many different-colored squares of cloth she had sewn together with her tired, drawn, tense fingers and stretched across the quilting frame. This had been left unfinished before going to give assistance to the Creefs. Quietly she sat down to quilt, but soon grew tired and weary as time moved along.

Silence filled the room as she knelt by the bedside to pray. The window shade beside the bed was raised high. She lay on the squeaky old wooden bed, her head on the long bolster, and watched the stars twinkle in the firmament. Soon she was locked in a sea of deep sleep.

Early the next morning, in the dim light of dawn, she suddenly awoke feeling somewhat less depressed than the night before. A mockingbird sat on a limb up in the scraggy dying apple tree only a few feet away from the kitchen door, and sang his morning song while Miss Nancy baked a small pan of biscuits. Steam rose from the perking old yaupon pot and filled the room.

Yaupon is a hollylike tree, or shrub. Indians, early settlers and

37

the natives along the Outer Banks used the leaves and tender twigs to make tea. It was their favorite drink and still is in some parts of northeastern North Carolina.

After breakfast she busied herself tidying the surroundings, which occupied her for only a short time although she moved about at a very slow pace. Heat from the brilliant late September sun caused her to feel more at ease while it rose over the dark, thick, cluster of trees as she huddled on the edge of the porch. Soon, in deep thought, Miss Nancy leaned back against the corner post.

Time stood still for her in this little world of isolated wilderness at East Lake. To her, now more than ever, life seemed long, lonely, and empty.

For the Creef family it had been a busy Fall. Rebecca and the children were kept very active peeling, coring, and preparing their excellent harvest of delicious Bartlett pears. Some pears were canned, some made into preserves, and some were stored and strawed over inside the potato house near the winter garden, to be eaten fresh just as they were after being carefully selected and picked by hand from the tree to prevent bruising.

Corncribs were full to the top. Large, round, deep-orange pumpkins sat side by side on the barn floor in a dark gloomy corner, ready to be made into delicious pumpkin pies. Three small barrels of salt spots and mullets rested against the wall. Wood to be burned in the clay-filled stone fireplace was racked shoulder-high along the back fence.

The harvest was over; it was the last week in October. The round yellow moon was full. Bright moonbeams shone down on the bare little patches where crops had been grown. Cottontail rabbits quietly hopped and played about. The harvest moon was always welcomed by everyone as it looked down on this drowsy, unfrequented village, casting on the ground dark shadows made by differently shaped objects.

Many moons had come and gone with little or no change, to communicate with the outside world. Already icy sparkling frost had colored the leaves on the trees near the house as well as in the wooded area. The wind suddenly shifted from a south to a northwesterly position. Black clouds drifted across the partly overcast sky. An early winter seemed likely, for the sting in the air was sharp.

Purple, gold, red, and orange leaves, all colors of the rainbow, rained down from the trees, mingled with the dust on the ground, and danced in every direction across the barnyard. A fine cold mist blew against their faces as Wash and Rebecca carried small logs from the woodpile and placed them on the porch against the wall to be burned as firewood in the open fireplace.

The mist changed to rain; it was a windy, rainy night in East Lake. After supper, the family left the kitchen and huddled in the living room in front of the logs burning on the hearth. Reflection from the bright blaze shone on their happy faces. Shadows of objects in the room danced on the walls, and burning embers flickered on the clay hearth.

For a while legends, ghost stories, and memories of the past began to come to life and live again as the Creefs chatted in an informal manner among themselves. But before long they all were snugly tucked in their beds the quilts pulled up about their necks.

Outside the wind seemed to intensify; it was a really stormy night. The northwest gale howled and roared as it grew stronger and complained among the leaves on the nearby trees. It whispered under the eaves of the house as the family listened to the popping, cracking noises of the rafters and standing timbers. Strong gusts of wind pushed against the old wood-frame, two-story house as the family drifted off to dreamland.

Some time in the early hours of the morning, falling rain turned into sleet. Through out the next day sharp, clear, loud honks were heard from flocks of wild Canadian geese, flying in a V formation, heading in the direction of the lake and marshes in search of food, water, and a haven.

By four o'clock in the afternoon the storm clouds had given way to a clear blue sky, leaving a strong steady wind blowing from the west. Wash quietly walked down the narrow hard-beaten path that led from the house along the edge of the field through the woods and on to the lake, where wild geese were busy feeding and talking in their language.

He crept slowly nearer the lake. In an opening between the trees and the lake he noticed that some of the geese were paddling at the shoreline, but too far to kill. Here he waited. Dusk soon settled over the area. Through long years of experience, Wash had learned that it was best to wait for the geese to move about and come close enough to be shot. Patiently he watched them through the gloom of twilight. Then as they came within range, he quietly raised his musket and fired.

At noon on the following day two young fat, tender-baked geese sat in the middle of the table in the kitchen. On one side of them sat a pan of juicy oven-baked sweet potatoes, syrup oozing out into the pan through the cracks in the peels. On the other side a plate of hot brown clabber biscuits rested near a bowl of steaming brown gravy. Two large pumpkin pies and a pound of homemade butter finished decorating the drab little table with food fit for a king.

Then came the sound of unforgettable footsteps on the back porch. Rebecca quickly smiled as she glanced at Wash, then rushed toward the kitchen door.

Loneliness had created in Miss Nancy a strong urge to return to the Creefs for a short afternoon visit. The family had missed her, and welcomed her with open arms. She had come just in time for a wonderful rich meal. It required little effort on Rebecca's part to persuade Miss Nancy to spend the night with them.

Later, once more all were gathered around the open fireplace to watch the bright soft glow and feel the warmth from the logs burning on the hearth while the gray smoke curled and streaked up the chimney.

Large, fluffy, light kernels of popcorn were popped over the open flame and enjoyed by all. Miss Nancy was very happy as she sat and rocked little George while he slept. Tonight she appeared to be in an intermediate position; maybe because during the past two weeks she had been carefully examining and studying the holy scriptures on the brown, worn, faded pages of the old family Bible. Tomorrow would be her birthday; seventy-three years old, and still normally active.

As they munched on the popcorn, making a crunching sound, she said, "What a wonderful savior Jesus was, to come to this sin-cursed world and take our place on the Cross so we can have life eternal. Just think, though two thousand years have passed since the Resurrection of Jesus, He still lives and stands forth today and always, proclaimed by God, acknowledge by the angles, adored by the saints, and feared by the devils. For there is only one mediator between God and man, and this man is

Jesus Christ. The mornings, the evenings, the sun, moon, and stars in the heavens, declare his glory and shout. Truly," Miss Nancy went on, "I can say tonight that He lives, for He lives in my heart."

The light from the burning embers on the hearth made the tears glitter as they slowly trickled down her wrinkled face. She gazed steadily at the precious little bundle in her arms. Silence once more filled the room. God had spoken to her, just as He speaks to all of us today. But how many of us listen as Miss Nancy did?

Rebecca and Wash glanced briefly at each other, they were greatly moved. They knew that more than ever before, the lonely hours Miss Nancy had spent in solitude for the past two weeks had had a great emotional effect on her.

Early next morning, Miss Nancy began the one-mile journey back home. Slowly she walked along the narrow dirt road. Birds sang their morning songs and fluttered about close by in the branches of trees. Squirrels sat on their haunches close under the trees, and chatted at each other while acorns bounced on the leaves as they fell from the oak trees. Many beautiful colored leaves covered the ground, adding richness and splendor to the natural Autumn scenery along this primitive little universe.

Her footsteps began to slow as she moved on, almost winded and out of breath. Around the last winding bend in the road she sat down to rest.

Many happenings in the past while she had walked among mankind in this isolated village during the past seventy-three years came to visit her as she sat meditating by the side of the road. The hands of time were closing in; she became extremely melancholy and wept before dozing off.

The cooing of a turtledove on a tree branch above her head broke the silence around her, and she awoke. More and more she felt the need of a companion as she drew nearer the sunset-flushed path, where little pink-and -yellow mixed late Fall flowers grew and blossomed along the trail that led to the front steps of her sleepy little hut. Crows cawed overhead, and flew low in a winding course over the pine thicket toward their roosting place for the night.

Miss Nancy's shoes were dusty and badly worn. She climbed

41

the steps to the porch. To relax after the exertion, she sat down in an old rocking chair that stood beside the wall.

Now, more than ever, she knew that the time had come for her to be more content with her loneliness. Never before had she felt so exhausted from this short walk that she had made so many, many times before. Suddenly she paused, her sad, tired, suntanned, wrinkled face turned westward, and she was amazed at the scenery.

Today it seemed to her more authentic than ever as magnificent sunbeams burst through the openings in the trees, and glorious streams of gold shone with a long slant across the yard. A large, round, red-and-gold ball, hung slightly above the treetops and was slowly descending. Sunlight was passing; another day was ending.

Mysterious shadows of the dark-green cedars, live oaks and pines that stood in the distance began merging on the ground. Then the gray gloom of twilight faded, and stars began to appear in the heavens. More and more Miss Nancy felt the burden of life that rides with the passing of time.

Going indoors, she moved cautiously across the small room toward the bed, feeling as though she would never make it. Finally she eased down on her soft featherbed and gently pulled the quilts up over her shoulder. Miss Nancy was not well. To her, the rest of the world seemed to be dead. Here, alone in her humble little home, she was very depressed and lonely.

The howling of the wind around the corner, and the whispering, soft, rustling sounds in the pines nearby soon lulled her to sleep.

It was Friday, November 29, 1856.

During the following Sunday morning services there was a sudden pause among the natives when the preacher called their attention to the fact that Miss Nancy's place was vacant. Why? She was very faithful to the little church, and was always there on time.

After the morning worship, Rebecca worried about her. With very little effort she persuaded Wash to drive the horse and cart to the quiet, secluded shack and take Miss Nancy home with them for dinner. To the Creef family, she was like one of them and they missed her very much. A strong northwest wind nipped at their fingers and turned their cheeks rosy as old Nag jogged along at his usual pace. On they went, and in a jiffy the little shack came in sight. Only the noise made by the movement of the cart wheels along the narrow dirt road, and the rattle of the chains on the cart shafts, could be heard as they came within a short distance of the house.

Everyone listened, and tried to get a glimpse of Miss Nancy. The late Fall sun shone very brightly, but the icy chill from the gusty and unfriendly northwest wind began to numb their fingers.

No sign of life. No smoke curled from the chimney. A strange feeling crept over Wash as he hitched Nag to the shambles of the weatherbeaten hitching post at the edge of the yard. After hesitating a few moments, hoping that Miss Nancy had seen them, Wash stepped down from the cart and strolled toward the front door.

Except for the soft rustling sound made by the wind in the pines as they bowed back and forth near the yard, a hovering stillness filled the air encircling the whole environment. Wash stared at Rebecca, after several knocks on the door brought no response. According to the small group of natives at the Sunday morning services, no one had seen Miss Nancy since the Friday before.

Leaving the shabby and worn door, Wash moved with caution across the loose weak boards to the edge of the sagging porch near the corner of the little shack. Moments later, a few steps away from the porch, he stopped beside her bedroom window. But more knocks still brought no reply.

The answer came as Wash raised the window from the outside and peered in. Then slowly he bowed his head and removed his hat. Rebecca burst into tears as she helped the children into the cart and hurried to the nearest neighbor for help. Wash sat on the chopping block at the woodpile and waited. In a short time some of the villagers arrived.

Miss Nancy had been respected and loved by young and old alike. She had been the so-called "Granny woman" for almost every baby born in this now sad and stranded spot on East Lake. All the younger generations knew her and loved her as they would a mother.

Many times she had stayed in the neighbors' homes and helped when the children's mothers were ill, and their fathers were out on fishing trips or hunting for food in the wild wooded areas.

Parson Lewis took charge of the situation. A small amount of daylight came through the little window in the poorly lighted room. Over in the dim, gloomy, far corner of the bedroom, under some old dusty clothing, they found a pear-shaped box unknown to anyone except to Miss Nancy. For this special occasion, she had prepared it to make it easier for everyone when the final curtain was lowered.

While the women were busy inside, the men dug a shallow grave in the family graveyard near the house. Children ran in every direction, gathering beautiful late-fall flowers which grew wild in the fence-locks and along the roadside and ditchbanks away from the bitter sting of the frosty winds. Flowers of many colorful shades, yellow, pink, purple, red, and orange were made into wreaths. A short simple burial followed. Miss Nancy had never married, and was the last of her family to be laid to rest beside her mother.

Some of the wildflowers were dug up by the roots and imbedded in the soil around the grave. Many tears were shed while hymns were sung. Each person hesitated for a few moments before leaving. Now there would be no more loneliness for Miss Nancy. They prayed that she was safe in the arms of her savior.

Rebecca turned once more toward the cold, drooping little shack. Ivy vines partially covered the slowly crumbling, clay-filled chimney and ran in all directions almost to the top. Dark evergreen leaves moved silently in the light breeze. Not a word was spoken when she turned and walked away, tears running down her sad drawn face. Wash helped her into the cart.

This was a great loss to the people of the village.

Today beautiful wild fall flowers that blossom in many shades and colors just before frost, still grow and thrive in this same lonely spot on Miss Nancy's grave. The wind still whispers overhead in the pines, and murmurs among the leaves in the branches of the scraggy old evergreen live oak trees, which still stand at the edge of the dense forest nearby.

Chapter Four

Confusion, Poverty, and Ruin

It was a cold rainy April on East Lake. The intense, bitter Winter had passed. Today, for the first time in a week, the sun shone brightly on the scattered low rooftops in the village. After a long day, busy putting in new planks in the side of his fishing boat on the shore, Wash started for home.

With the reins from Nag's bridle over his shoulder, he led the way. They entered a grove of cedars mixed with long-leaf pines and live oaks. Large low branches shaded the wide path as they walked along. The last rays of the setting sun sent golden shafts through the openings in the leaves. Twittering quail caused excitement as they darted across the path. From a treetop above, a robin sang his evening song. The air was still, and smelled fresh after being washed by the heavy April rains. The murmur of flowing water in the stream by the side of the path was pleasing to his ears as he walked at a leisurely pace toward the back gate, Nag following close behind.

Rebecca had also been on the move, doing the usual spring cleaning in the house, baking sweet potatoes, and preparing supper. She was watching closely through the kitchen window when Wash and Nag came into sight in the gloomy shadow of the trees at the edge of the field. Supper was almost ready. She began at once to bustle about, hurrying to and fro, setting the table that stood waiting against the wall by the window.

The smell of juicy, baking sweet potatoes was in the air as Wash led Nag near the back porch on their way to the moss-covered watering trough. By the time Wash had finished feeding and watering his livestock, Rebecca had milked the cow. Supper was waiting. The family gathered around the table, gave thanks to their Maker, and before long the meal was over.

Rebecca loved the springtime of the year, when everything was beginning to bud, blossom, leaf out, and live again. Early the next morning she fixed breakfast while Wash and the children were getting ready. Nag was hitched to the cart, and then he pulled the whole family down to the shore along the lake where the repaired boat was ready to be put back into the water.

By noon old Nag had pulled the boat through the sand and was wading out in the water, dragging the boat behind him. As soon as the boat began to float, Wash turned Nag around and he waded back to shore.

Jumping mullets were playing in the water near the shore. This Spring was the most beautiful one they had seen in many years. Plenty of rain showers mixed with the warmth from the sun made the undergrowth flourish; it grew vigorously everywhere.

Wash loaded the family into his boat and hoisted the sail. They were all going for a boat ride on this beautiful Spring day. Nag would wait, hitched to a low evergreen bush, and stood chewing on the leaves as the boat sailed around the marsh and out of sight.

Spring was really bursting out and could not go unnoticed as they entered the canal from the lake. Moss, ferns, and lilies overhung its green banks. Around them rose tender marsh sage, and lofty green foliage waved back and forth in the gusty southeast wind.

Kingfishers darted, uttering loud piercing cries. Wild ducks that dotted the lake were eating grass seeds; blue herons stood motionless at the water's edge, and red-wing blackbirds sang their song swinging on tall sage stalks along the shady banks of the lake as gulls and fish hawks sailed above. From the trees and shrubs came the song of the robins.

Wash gazed at Rebecca and thought how much she loved the birds, the green of the trees, grass, and the lovely colorful flowers of springtime.

They listened to the flow of the water making a bubbling, rippling sound against the broad sides of the boat as it glided along through the cool amber-colored water of the lake. Then slowly the tiller was pushed to one side, moving the rudder and turning the boat around toward home.

About half a mile down the lake was a luxuriant growth of cypress and juniper trees that now slowly came in sight through an open space covered with deep, soft, green grass. The scenery was magnificent. Such peaceful surroundings.

The hot summers, the cool falls, icy winters, and budding springs, each in all its beauty came and went as the hands of time moved on. Then, in 1861, a state of mental distress hovered over this great nation—trouble between the states over slavery. Many slaves were gradually freed in several parts of the United States. In 1860, there were more than thirty thousand free Negroes in the state of North Carolina. Also in 1860, there were three thousand, five hundred and fifty free Negroes who owned property, some in the amount of thirty-six thousand dollars each. And, strange as it may seem, a few free Negroes themselves owned slaves. In 1830, two free Negroes owned forty-four slaves each. But there were still plenty of slaves to be freed.

President Lincoln felt it his duty to preserve the Union. When this long, bloody, costly war began, Lincoln called on North Carolina for troops to fight against the Confederacy. But Governor John W. Ellis, from Rowan County, replied No! If North Carolina must fight, it would fight for and not against the South.

Again during this period of unrest in 1862, Governor Zebulon B. Vance, the next Governor of North Carolina, expressed the feelings of most North Carolinians when he said, "If war must come, I prefer to be with my own people. If we have to shed blood, I prefer to shed Northern rather than Southern blood."

During the first year of the Civil War, North Carolina was greatly neglected by Jefferson Davis who was President of the Confederate States—neglected by not sending help and letting the North get control of the sounds of Eastern North Carolina which opened the waterway to Norfolk, Virginia.

Wilmington ports and Weldon railroads, which led to the rear of General Robert E. Lee's Army, were also controlled by the North. United States ships seized Hatteras Inlet, Roanoke Island, Fort Macon at Beaufort, New Bern, and the eastern part of the state.

Blockade runners brought in supplies for the Confederacy through the port of Wilmington from Nassau and other West Indian ports. Many people agreed with Governor Vance when he stated it was "a rich man's war, and a poor man's fight."

For half a century the history of the United States was a prelude to the bloody conflict between the states, which we call the Civil War. Then, for four heart-breaking years, brother fought brother. A fire had been kindled which all the waters of the

47

oceans could not put out, and which only a sea of blood could extinguish, so that ardent Howell Cobb from Georgia told Congress during the debates on the slavery question that led to the famous Missouri Compromise. Perhaps few of his listeners believed in his prophecy, but he was right; for through one of the bloodiest of all wars was the slavery question in the United States laid to rest, at least for almost a century. Now the racial unrest in the United States is at its peak. Will the educational systems, for which our forefathers fought and established, be destroyed? Ask yourselves why good has bowed to evil; why have our government leaders become so weak as to let our nation become involved so deeply in foreign affairs and bleed this nation financially, shed unnecessary blood, seem to fail to see the light, and walk in total darkness.

Undoubtedly the slavery question lay at the bottom of the first murderous struggle. It is true, of course, that the North and the South did not agree on the interpretation of the Constitution. On most issues, the North was content to permit the national government to expand its powers because, through national bounty, these sections had gained much—and they still have much to gain.

The South, however, objected to this gradual expansion of national powers, and pinned its faith to the doctrine of states' rights. A protective tariff might aid the Northern manufacturer; but the South was almost wholly agricultural and wished to trade its produce, particularly cotton, for cheap foreign goods.

Also the program of internal improvement, which was so essential to the prosperity of the North, meant far less to the South, where the seacoast was relatively close at hand and river systems were also numerous.

The policy of giving public lands to the landless failed to interest the Southern planters, since it was so clearly designed to aid the free farmer rather than the master of the slaves. Southern statesmen reasoned that the expansion of national powers need not and must not be permitted. If the national government arrogated too much power to itself, they held that the states, having themselves created the Union, might lawfully withdraw from the Union. The doctrine of states' rights would hardly have been cherished so deeply had the institution of slavery played a less important part in the economic life of the South.

George Washington Creef, Jr.

One of the Wonders of the World:
The largest and oldest grapevine in America

Roanoke Island, North Carolina
The best fish in the country are caught here.

INDIANS COOKING FISH. Usually the fish were cooked on racks insured thorough cooking of the larger fish. The waters at Island were full of fish, and the forests were rich in fruit and Raleigh's early colonists called the Roanoke Island section the under the cope of Heaven."

Two Young Indian Warriors

An Indian Village

Early Settler Defends Home and Family

Blackbeard, the Pirate

BLACKBEARD. Edward Teach, or Thatch, commonly called Blackbeard, operated as a pirate off North Carolina for only a few months before he was killed near Ocracoke Island by Captain Robert Maynard of the Royal Navy.

Wild Ponies of the Outer Banks

Eleanor Dare Holding Her Daughter, Virginia
(A scene from the "Lost Colony".)

Birthplace of George Washington Creef, Jr.
The old home, now in ruins, is over 200 years old.

Miss Nancy's Shack at East Lake, N. C.

Wrecked Schooner on Outer Banks

Abraham Lincoln

Theodosia Burr, Pirates' Victim(?) (January,

Theodosia Burr, Daughter of Aaron Burr,
Her mysterious disappearance has never been solved.

Yeopon Bushes on Roanoke Island
Yeopon tea is a favorite drink of natives of the Outer Banks.

Home of Early Settlers on Outer Banks

Log Cabin on Historic Roanoke Island

Odd-shaped Cypress Knees Near the Shore

Cape Hatteras Lighthouse

Bodie Island Lighthouse, Now Part of Cape Hatteras National Park

Part of the Vines at Mother Vineyard

George Washington Creef's Home in Manteo
This is where he died, February 10, 1928.

Jockey Ridge Sand Hill in Background
This pile at Nag's Head, N. C. is the tallest along the Atlantic Coast.

Another View of Jockey Ridge

Slavery was actually introduced in Virginia in 1619, and was legal before the Revolutionary War in all the colonies in the north as well as in the south. The law, however, flourished mostly in the Southern colonies, where slaves could be used profitably as field laborers in the cultivation of tobacco, cotton, potatoes, and corn.

When the American Revolution broke out, three-fourths of the Negroes lived south of the Mason-Dixon line. During the early years of American national history, slavery was looked upon as a dying institution. By the year of 1804, the seven northernmost states of the original thirteen had abolished slavery, and talk of freeing the slaves was common even in Virginia, Maryland, and Delaware.

After the originators of the Constitution finally agreed that slave trade should be prohibited in 1808, they could have assumed that they had paved the way for the ultimate extinction of slavery because they believed that the institution could not live without the importation of new slaves.

Leading American statesmen were openly hostile to the continuation of slavery. George Washington freed his slaves by his own will; Benjamin Franklin and Alexander Hamilton belonged to emancipation societies; Thomas Jefferson wrote his antislavery views into the Northwest Ordinance of 1787. Except among a few small groups, such as the Quakers, opposition to slavery did not rest on moral but rather on social and economic grounds.

The danger from insurrections was deemed great; the existence of slavery tended to lower and discourage free labor. The profits from slave holdings were uncertain, except under the most favorable conditions. Even during the years that the cotton gin was working, a revolution in Southern agricultural states and profits from slavery were easing the minds of the Southerners as to the evils of the system.

Democratic doctrines were sweeping the Western frontier and the industrial centers of the East. Not only was political equality demanded for all men, but reforms of a social and economic nature were also being preached. Demands for free public education, the rights of women, better wages and working conditions for the laborers, more human treatment of criminals and the insane, world peace, and the gospel preached among the

49

heathens were heard on every hand. Of course this was a lot of wishful thinking—easier said than done.

It was most certain that this crusading would presently attack the slavery system in the South with its utter denial of the most basic human rights.

The early movement for ending slavery in the United States had dwindled to unimportance after 1808. But in 1831, William Loyd Garrison revived the agitation by publishing in Boston a radical antislavery sheet known as the *Liberator*. Then, within a few years, abolitionist newspapers, orators, and magazines were common throughout the North. Some were extremely scornful of the Federal Constitution because it legalized and condoned slavery.

In 1836, Wendell Phillips, one of England's ablest orators, abandoned the law because his conscience would not permit him to take the oath to support the Constitution and thereafter lent his powerful voice to the abolitionist cause.

About the same time James G. Birney, an ex-planter and slaveholder, moved from Kentucky to Ohio. He tried to band together the antislavery forces into a political unit, the Liberty Party.

Among other notable recruits for the cause were the Quaker poet, John Greenleaf Whittier, and Theodore Parker, a preacher. For a long time, however, even in the north, the abolitionists were a small minority. The offices of the abolitionist printers were regularly plundered. Elijah P. Lovejoy, of Alton, Illinois, was murdered when he tried to protect his property against an attacking mob.

Business in the north as a whole was against the reform, because trade with the South was good and abolitionist agitation might lessen it. Also, in the northwest, many ex-Southerners, who although happy enough to get away from the slavery system, were convinced that the primitive Negroes were not fit for freedom.

Most of the antislavery advocates had no firsthand knowledge of the institution they criticized, and their statements were often untrue. Southerners, who before this time might have doubted the wisdom of slavery, now began to defend it—not merely as a necessary evil, but as a righteous and benevolent institution. The Southerners compared it with the "wage-slave" system, which the Northerners were using in their factories, and some convinced themselves that under slavery the laborer was better cared for than under the free-labor system.

Preachers proclaimed that slavery was sanctioned by the Ten Commandments, and this was accepted in the Southern churches. The ministers claimed that it was in the teachings of Jesus, and clearly ordained of God. Southern politicians raged frantically against the abolitionist petitions that were continually being presented before Congress and the House of Representatives. They secured the passage of a "gag resolution," which required that all petitions concerning slavery be laid on the table without reading or discussion.

This blow at the constitutional right of freedom of petition angered ex-President John Quincy Adams, who now, as a member of the House, had endeared himself to the antislavery element by his valiant fight against the rule.

The abolitionists won very few wholeheartedly by their teachings, but they did convince many Northerners that slavery should not be allowed to spread. The first result of this conviction was the Missouri Compromise in 1820. The admission of Texas to the Union in 1845, and the acquisition of a great section of territory from Mexico in the War of 1846 to 1848, seemed to open new opportunities for slavery to spread.

For a time the North and South were on the verge of war; but after the Compromise of 1850, Congress made another effort to satisfy all parties to the dispute. Perhaps the most dangerous provision in this compromise was a drastic measure for the return of fugitive slaves.

Many antislavery men openly scorned this law. They set up "underground railroads" with stations in homes of sympathizers where runaway slaves might rest, be fed and directed by guides to the next stop on their journey to Canada and freedom.

Some of the Northern states also passed "personal liberty laws," which went as far as they could toward preventing the enforcement of the national Fugitive Slave Act. The compromise of 1850, through the effort of Henry Clay, did not kill Southern determination to acquire further territory for slavery expansion.

In 1854, James Buchanan, John Mason, and Pierre Soule, three American ministers, were sent to European capitals, and met at Ostend, Belgium, at President Pierce's request, to consider the problem of Cuba. It seemed as if Cuba had been attacked by expeditions aided or inspired by proslavery leaders.

The ministers issued the famous Ostend Manifesto, on October 9, in which they declared a measure necessary for the protection of slavery. They stated that Spain ought to sell Cuba to the United States; if Spain refused to sell, the island should then be taken by force.

That same year, 1854, Senator Stephen A. Douglas pushed through Congress his famous Kansas-Nebraska Act, repealing the Missouri Compromise, but three years later the Supreme Court held in the Dred Scott Decision that Congress had no right to prohibit slavery in any of the territories of the United States.

Now people insisted more and more on the moral aspects of the slavery issue. The doctrine that slavery was morally wrong, and that it ought to be started on the road to ultimate extinction won increasing support from the Northerners. There were some extremists—like John Brown, who in 1859 led the desperate raid on Harpers Ferry, which brought him a sentence of death by treason, and who was hanged at Harpers Ferry in Virginia.

Brown's plan had been to start a Negro insurrection in the South, by which the slaves could help with their own freedom. To many Northerners, this plan caused Brown to become a martyr; and the Southerners tended to ascribe his extreme views to even the most moderate antislavery men.

As the new Republican Party grew in strength, and as its prospects of winning control of the national government increased the South threatened more earnestly than ever before to secede from the Union. Then finally in 1860, the Republicans did win and they elected Abraham Lincoln as President. The Southern states, led by South Carolina, on December 20, 1860, carried out their threats, By February 1861, the seven states of the Lower South—South Carolina, Mississippi, Florida, Alabama, Georgia, Louisiana, and Texas—had seceded from the Union, formed a new government, and called themselves the Confederate States of America.

Jefferson Davis and Alexander Hamilton Stephens, between November 6, 1860, the day Lincoln was elected, and March 4, 1861, the day he took office, made many efforts to preserve the Union. President James Buchanan (of Pennsylvania) was very much devoted to the Union, but most of his advisers had been Southerners and he refused on constitutional grounds to attempt the coercion of the South.

Perhaps this policy of inaction, which was also followed by Lincoln for several weeks after his inauguration, was as well calculated as any to induce the South to reconsider its decision. In Congress, many earnest men also sought a way out.

A Senate Committee of thirteen men, headed by Senator John J. Crittenden of Kentucky, prepared a compromise plan for a Constitutional amendment which provided that the Missouri Compromise line be extended to the Pacific Ocean. Also that Congress be prohibited from interfering with slavery in land still under territorial status below 36° 30', and that the federal government pay for runaway slaves rescued in the North and refrain from prohibiting the transportation of slaves between states and territories.

Had this plan been adopted, it might have postponed the war. But Seward, the leading Republican member of the House Committee, consulted President Lincoln, who refused to support the compromise because it left the way open for the expansion of slavery.

Another effort for peace was made by the Virginia Legislature, which issued a call for a conference of states to be held in Washington on February 4. Ex-President John Tyler was chosen Chairman. Delegates were present from seven slaveholding and fourteen free states.

The conference recommended that Congress pass various acts making concessions to the slaveholding states. But Congress disregarded all the suggestions, and instead passed an amendment to the Constitution—which was offered by Senator Douglas—providing that Congress should never interfere with slavery in the states. The amendment was not ratified by the necessary number of states, and was quickly forgotten when the fighting began.

When Lincoln took office, he was careful to avoid all threats of war against the seceding South. But he declared that he would use his constitutional authority to hold the property and places in the South which belonged to the United States government.

Fort Sumter, an island stronghold at the mouth of Charleston harbor, was held by a small United States garrison. On April 6, Lincoln ordered the *Star of the West* to proceed with food for the garrison, and at the same time he notified Governor Pickens of South Carolina about his plans.

When the South learned of this decision, the bombardment of Fort Sumter was decided on. The small steamer was turned back by heavy fire from land batteries, but on April 12, 1861, the bombardment of the fort began. The garrison surrendered the next day. To everyone's sorrow, the Civil War had begun.

Until the time Fort Sumter was fired on, many people in the North and the South had been determined to prevent war at any cost. Some Northerners, including Horace Greeley, editor of the influential New York *Tribune,* had argued that Lincoln should "let the erring sisters go in peace." Many Southerners had opposed secession, and in some of the seceding states the decision to leave the Union was made only after a very close vote. The bombardment of Fort Sumter, however, ended all hope of peace.

Lincoln at once called on the loyal states to furnish him with 75,000 state militia. President Davis issued a proclamation for 100,000 volunteers from the Confederate States. At this moment, both sections were excited and eager for the conflict.

Virginia, North Carolina, Tennessee, and Arkansas now joined the seceding South, while four border states—Maryland, Delaware, Kentucky, and Missouri—stayed with the North. Some of the western counties of Virginia, where the hold of slavery had never been, soon broke away from the "Old Dominion" and, in 1863, joined the Union as the State of West Virginia.

In the division of strength, the North fared far better than the South. Only eleven states left the Union, and twenty-two remained loyal. The population of the loyal states was about 22,000,000 and that of the seceding states was less than 10,000,000 of whom more than a third were slaves. In fighting strength, the men in the North outnumbered the South three to one; and in wealth, not less than two to one.

The North had every type of industry within its borders, including 92 percent of the total manufacturing of the nation and most of its mineral resources. The South was chiefly agricultural, with an abnormal dependence on the production of cotton.

To the North fell most of the United States Navy and most of the privately owned merchant vessels, thus making possible virtual control of the high seas in the interest of the Union. The North also had a decided advantage in the means of land communications, for it had more than twice as many miles of railroads as the South, including several lines only lately completed, which tended to bind the Northwest and the Northeast closely together.

The North also possessed the means of maintaining the effectiveness of its railroads, and the South did not. The railroad situation was more important than contemporaries realized.

The Civil War was the first great war in which the railroads furnished the chief means of transporting troops and supplies from place to place. With all this preponderance or power of assets on its side, the astonishment was not that the North won but rather how the South was able to resist for so long.

Neither side was prepared for war, and during the first year and a half of the struggle the chief concern of both the North and South was to create armies. The overconfident Union forces under General Irvin McDowell were defeated in the first clash of arms at Bull Run, or Manassas, on July 21, 1861, by Confederate troops of Generals Joseph E. Johnston and Pierre Beauregard. Through this defeat the North learned two lessons that came home to them, also to the South.

First, that the war could not be fought without trained soldiers; and second, that the conflict would probably last for a long time. In the beginning, both sides raised troops only by volunteering. But in 1862, the South resorted to compulsory service. In 1863, the North passed a draft act which could be invoked in any district where the number of volunteers was deemed inadequate.

Both sides had great difficulty at first in equipping their troops. Northern factories soon solved that problem for the Union; and importations from Europe, despite the blockades, brought the Southern armies to great effectiveness.

Then federal successes under General George B. McClellan in Western Virginia helped keep that doubtful territory in the Union. Meanwhile, in Missouri the efforts of Captain Nathaniel Lyon, Francis P. Blair and the two younger Blairs, aided by slight military successes of the Union forces under General Fremont, held that state in the Union. Kentucky, under Governor Beriah Magoffin, attempted to remain neutral and demanded the withdrawal of both Union and Confederate troops. Bishop Leonidas Polk, the General who was commanding the Confederates, refused to withdraw unless General Grant, who had just occupied Paducah, withdrew first.

A convention in November 1862, passed an ordinance of secession; but during most of the war the major part of the state was actually held by Union troops. As in the World War of 1914-1918, the Civil War developed two battlefronts; one in the east, and the other in the west. The campaigns in the east were fought mainly in Virginia and Maryland, with each army intent on the capture of the opposing capital.

General McClellan, the first Union Commander in the east, proved to be a great drillmaster but a timid warrior. He was easily outmaneuvered and defeated by General Robert E. Lee, a great leader of the Southern forces and who displayed the highest type of military genius.

In the Peninsular Campaign of 1862, McClellan aimed to bring his forces by water as far as Fortress Monroe, and then reach Richmond by crossing the narrow peninsula between the York and James rivers. McDowell's troops, held at Fredericksburg in defense of Washington, were to provide reinforcements if needed.

But the Army of the Potomac was delayed for a month, besieging Yorktown. When it had reached a position on the Chickahominy, ready to attack the Confederate capital, McDowell was ordered away to the Shenandoah Valley. There "Stonewall" Jackson's foot cavalry in a lightning campaign had defeated Northern troops under Banks and Milroy, and had advanced to Harpers Ferry where they seemed to threaten Washington. After making this threat, Jackson hurried his men by train to the defense of Richmond. Here General Lee had sent General J. E. B. Stuart on a brilliant raid during which his hard-riding cavalry had entirely circled McClellan's forces, destroyed many supplies, and brought back information that aided General Lee to take the offensive and drive McClellan back in the seven-day battle which ended at Malvern Hill, July 1, 1862.

President Lincoln now placed General Henry Halleck in command of all Union armies. He ordered General McClellan to abandon his dangerous position south of Richmond, and to unite with the federal forces in Northern Virginia under the command of General John Pope.

Lee hurried north to strike Pope before enforcements could arrive. Then another daring Stuart raid brought him Pope's dispatch book containing Pope's plans, and still another forced march by Jackson's men destroyed Pope's supply base at

Manassas Junction. Then Pope's troops, pursuing Jackson's, unexpectedly found themselves facing General Lee's entire army. They were thoroughly routed in the second Battle of Bull Run which took place on August 28, 29, and 30. Then they retired within the defense of Washington.

General Robert E. Lee and his army now crossed the Potomac River to invade Maryland, his object being partly to transfer the fighting to northern soil and also to influence the coming Fall elections in the North.

When he found that a strong garrison at his rear at Harpers Ferry threatened his communications, he sent more than half his forces under Jackson to capture that fort on September 15, 1862.

Meanwhile McClellan, having obtained a copy of General Lee's general orders, advanced with his troops and caused Lee to withdraw his remaining divisions behind Antietam Creek. Now while McClellan hesitated for a day and made reconnaissances, Jackson with his three divisions was making a forced night march from Harpers Ferry. When the Union troops attacked on the morning of September 17 they met Lee's forces reunited, except for Hill's division which was guarding the captured Harpers Ferry garrison.

The Union victory at Antietam, slight though it was, gave President Lincoln the opportunity to issue the Emancipation Proclamation, decreeing the freedom of all slaves in territory still in rebellion.

January 1, 1863, the President took this momentous step to introduce a new moral aim into the Northern cause that should spur enlistments and enthusiasm, and hope to prevent intervention by foreign countries.

Then began Lincoln's search, which lasted for more than a year, for a general to cope with General Lee, who was outsmarting the Northern Generals.

With Burnside in command, the Army of the Potomac suffered a disastrous defeat at Fredericksburg on December 12, 1862. "Fighting Joe" Hooker fared but little better at Chancellorsville on May 23, 1863.

"Stonewall" Jackson, next to General Lee, was the ablest of the Southern officers. His death was a severe blow to the Confederacy. But in spite of Jackson's death, Lee again invaded the North.

At Gettysburg on July 1, 2, and 3, 1863, the tide of Southern success was at last turned. But General George Meade, the Union commander who had succeeded Hooker just on the eve of the battle, failed to follow up his victory with the kind of vigor that was badly needed at this time and so possibly lost a good chance to end the war.

On the western front, in the meantime, the Union commanders had a double objective: One was to clear the Mississippi of Confederate control, all the way to its mouth, and, by so doing, it would cut off the Confederate states west of the river from all effective participation in the war. The other was to advance the Union lines through Tennessee into the very heart of the South, and crush out all resistance as they went. From the first, better success attended the Union efforts in the West than in the East as early as February of 1862. When General Ulysses S. Grant began to advance into Tennessee, he captured Fort Donelson on the Tennessee River with the help of Commodore Foote and his gunboats.

Then he crossed to take Fort Donelson on the Cumberland River, after a desperate battle at Shiloh, on April 6 and 7, 1862. When the Southern leader, General Albert S. Johnson, was mortally wounded, he cut the Confederate railway communications with the East at Corinth, Mississippi. While the battle of Shiloh was being fought, General Pope's men and Foote's gunboats seized Island Number Ten, an important Confederate fort on the Mississippi River.

A few weeks later, Commodore David Farragut, with the help of an oceangoing fleet, ran the batteries at the mouth of the Mississippi River and paved the way for the occupation of New Orleans by the Union troops on May 1, 1862.

It was not until more than a year later, however, that the Federals rolled unvexed to the sea, leaving behind destruction in every way possible.

Then on July 4, 1863, just as the victory at Gettysburg was being celebrated throughout the north, came the news that Grant had taken Vicksburg after a desperate siege. Five days later, Port Hudson, the the only remaining Confederate river fort, surrendered.

Meanwhile the Southern Army of Tennessee had not been idle. In July 1862, a raiding party under General John Morgan had robbed, killed, and destroyed in central and eastern Kentucky, and even swept across Kentucky into Indiana and Ohio, in July 1863, before their defeat and capture.

Other raiders under Colonel Nathan Forrest destroyed federal stores and lines of communications in Tennessee. On October 8, General W. S. Rosecrans, now in command of the Confederate Army of the Cumberland, began pushing the Confederates eastward, then through Tennessee.

At Murfreesboro, on the Stone River, a bloody three-day battle was fought, which ended January 2, 1863. Battle after battle was fought against a superior Union force led by General William Sherman, fighting the battles of Resaca, Dallas, and Kenesaw Mountain.

General Grant was now called east to match his wits against those of the famous General Robert E. Lee, and the war entered into its final phase. As a tactician, there was no doubt that General Lee was far superior to General Grant; but by this time the Confederate forces were beginning to dwindle. The Northern losses, however heavy, were being immediately made good.

During the year 1864, Grant forced the fighting in a campaign of attrition. The battle of the Wilderness on May 5 and 6, 1864, Spottsylvania on May 8 through 12, 1864, and Cold Harbor on June 1 through 3, 1864, were bloody but inconclusive. Grant then captured Petersburg, which was a very important railroad junction to the south of Richmond.

General Lee sent General Jubal Early raiding in the Shenandoah Valley, hoping to repeat Jackson's success of 1862; but General "Phil" Sheridan's cavalry troops routed him and ravaged the valley to destroy Confederate food and ammunition supplies. By now Sherman's army had captured Atlanta on September 2, 1864, and had marched on to the sea leaving in its path waste and destruction almost sixty miles wide.

General Sherman reached Savannah, Georgia, on December 20, 1864, then turned northward to join forces with Grant. But before that could happen, General Lee, with a small army, his supplies exhausted and his back to the wall, surrendered on April 9, 1865, after the fall of Richmond, at Appomattox Court House in Virginia.

General Joseph Johnston, whose army had made contact with Sherman's in North Carolina, surrendered to Sherman, after several bloody battles, on April 26, 1865, at the Bennett house, three miles went of Durham. The war was over.

Whether right or wrong, some historians may affirm the fact that the main factor in defeating the Confederacy was not the Northern armies, but rather the Northern blockade. Early in the war Lincoln proclaimed a blockade of the entire Southern coastline, and by pressing every conceivable kind of ship into use the blockade became reasonably effective. But blockade runners did indeed get through, and, thanks to them, as well as to the fact that an enormous amount of trade through the military lines was licensed, the Southern Armies were able to carry on as long as they did. Efforts on the part of the South to break the blockade were useless.

The Confederacy expected a great deal from the ironclad *Merrimac*. These ships were constructed at the Norfolk Navy Yard, but the famous battle with the *Monitor*, on March 9, 1862, put an end to these hopes. Several commerce destroyers, built in England for the Confederacy, did much damage to Northern commerce on the high seas but nothing toward breaking the blockade. Some ironclad rams, designed for the purpose of raising the blockade, were built in England; but due to the strenuous representations of the Minister to England, Charles Francis Adams, they never were permitted to sail.

Gradually the Union captured the main Southern ports through which the blockade runners smuggled supplies to the Southern Armies. New Orleans was the first to be captured.

In the year of 1864, Farragut's warships took Mobile Harbor despite the defense of forts, mines, and Confederate ships. Early in 1865, Fort Fisher, guarding Wilmington's busy harbor, was stormed by Commander Porter's fleet cooperating with land forces under General Alfred H. Terry.

A little over a month later, Sherman's troops took Charleston. Many of the Northern citizens did not approve of the war, and bitterly opposed it. They organized themselves into secret societies, such as the Knights of the Golden Circle, and sought to embarrass the government by discouraging enlistments, opposing the draft, and even helping Confederate prisoners to escape.

They also criticized as unconstitutional all doubtful measures taken by the Lincoln Administration, such as the suspension of the writ of habeas corpus. They pointed to the inefficiency of President Lincoln and his advisers in the conduct of the war. They were outraged immeasurably by the Emancipation Proclamation, which, in their judgement, made the war only to free the slaves. They became extremely influential in the Democratic Party, and, in the elections of 1862, they scored important victories in such states as Illinois, Indiana, and Ohio. In 1864, peace-at-any-price men wrote the Democratic national platform; but the convention nominated General George McClellan as its candidate, and he came out in the open for winning the war.

Lincoln himself despaired of reelection; if it had not been for General Sherman's timely victories, he might have been defeated.

Another peril that the Northern government had to face was foreign intervention. The South definitely depended on this because the South believed that the European nations, particularly England, must have the cotton which was so necessary to the manufacturing industry and that, if necessary, they would help them fight the North for it.

Early in the war, the South dispatched two agents, Mason and Slidell, to England and France, respectively. They were taken from a British ship, and returned to the United States as prisoners. This incident nearly involved the United States and Great Britain in war.

There was also much trouble about the commerce destroyers, which the British government permitted to be built in the British shipyards. The most famous of these ships, the *Alabama*, commanded by Captain Raphael Semmes, took a heavy toll of Northern shipping. Other difficulties arose with reference to the enforcement of the blockade that the North maintained along the whole Southern Coast.

If the British aristocracy had had its way, England would certainly have recognized the independence of the Confederacy. But the lower class did not want war. However, when the British working people were finally convinced that the United States was fighting for the cause of free labor and against slave labor, their sympathies were all with the North.

England soon found other sources of supply for cotton, but her profits as a neutral, and her great need of Northern wheat would probably have been enough to discourage her from intervention in the Civil War.

France, at the time of the Civil War, under the rule of Napoleon III, was definitely unfriendly to the United States, and sponsored an expedition to Mexico with the object of making that republic a satellite state for France.

Now the great task that faced the United States at the close of the war was the reconstruction of the South. During the Civil War, heavy burdens were carried by every American. In 1862, bacon was thirty-three cents a pound; but in 1865, the price rose to seven and a half dollars a pound. Eggs rose from thirty-five cents to five dollars a dozen. Flour went from eighteen dollars to five hundred dollars a barrel. People were forced to use many kinds of substitutes, such as wood for shoes, wheat straw for hats, and parched corn for coffee.

Soldiers left the Army by the hundreds and thousands; some hid in the swamps and mountains. Already more than 40,000 of the finest men in North Carolina, ranging in age from sixteen to sixty had lost their lives; and thousands returned handicapped for life by the loss of an arm, leg, eye, or other injuries.

They returned after the war with no money, little food, livestock gone, buildings burned to the ground; Negro slaves were set free at once. The story was widespread in 1865 by the North that each freed man would get forty acres of land and a mule. However, Negroes who expected this gift were sadly disappointed because this was not true. As a whole, the situation was one of defeat, confusion, poverty, and ruin for both whites and Negroes.

In 1865, North Carolina set up a Bureau and it began its work to provide schools, food, clothing, and medicine for both white and black.

As far back as 1863, Abraham Lincoln announced his plan to pardon all Southerners except a few secession leaders. This plan pleased most Southerners. But Republican radicals disagreed with President Lincoln. Before he had time to apply his plan and to battle with the radicals in Congress, he was shot to death in a Washington theater by actor John Wilkes Booth.

Many Southerners knew they had lost a friend. Andrew Johnson, a native of North Carolina, became the next President of the

United States. He wanted to carry out most of Lincoln's plan. He was bold and able, but did not have the patience of Lincoln with those who opposed him.

At first the radicals liked Johnson because they thought that he would go along with them in their views about the treatment of the South. But when they learned that President Johnson's policies were quite similar to those of Lincoln, they came out to oppose him even more than they had opposed Lincoln.

Lincoln had assumed that since secession was unconstitutional it had never taken place, and that the Southern states were therefore still in the Union. President Johnson accepted this theory of state perdurance, and, following precedents set by Lincoln, he purposed to allow the citizens of each seceded state, whenever enough of them had taken the necessary oaths of allegiance to the United States, to reestablish their own governments. They must annul their ordinances of secession, repudiate the debts they had incurred in fighting the war, and also abolish slavery.

By December 1865, every Southern state except Texas had gone through this process, and, so far as Johnson was concerned each was entitled to its full rights in the Union.

Congress, however, led by Thaddeus Stevens in the House, and Charles Sumner in the Senate, refused to recognize Johnson's work and denied Southern Representatives and Senators seats in Congress. Stevens further held that the Southern states were only conquered provinces, the destiny of which Congress might now decide. Sumner argued that by the act of secession the Southern states had lost their rights and privileges in the Union. Both Sumner and Stevens insisted that Congress alone should decide how the Southern states should be reconstructed.

A long struggle began shaping up between the President and Congress, which followed immediately. Congress won, and the South was forced to submit to a second reconstruction.

The Congressional plan of reconstruction that was now substituted for President Johnson's plan involved several features extremely unpleasant, or offensive, to the South. Among them was military rule, during a probationary period; Negro suffrage; and the disfranchisement of nearly all the leading whites for treason. Working under these handicaps, new constitutions were formed by the ten unreconstructed states.

Tennessee had been readmitted in July 1866. By the summer of 1870, the last of them, Georgia, was back in the Union. The newly devised state governments were no longer in the hands of representative citizens. Most of the offices were held by illiterate Negroes who were uneducated; many of them could not even read or write. Many were Northern adventurers—called carpetbaggers because they came South with all their worldly possessions in carpetbags. The Southern whites who had not supported the South in its struggle for independence were called scalawags.

Naturally an overindulgence in activities and wild merrymaking of government corruption followed in which the prostrate South was plundered. The Negroes that were organized by the carpetbaggers not only voted as they were told, but they also became an unbearable and severe social menace to their former masters. These conditions gave roots to such secret orders of Southern whites as the Klu Klux Klan, which was aimed to frighten the freed Negroes and their white leaders into a decent respect for the rights of their fellow citizens.

Later a few laws passed by Congress on February 28, 1870, placed elections in the reconstructed states under national control, and a force bill, passed on April 20, 1871, authorized the President to use the Army in suppressing the Southern secret societies. But the Negro menace was never again formidable.

As for the carpetbag governments, they lasted only so long as federal troops were kept in the South. Just as soon as the threat of force was gone, Southern white men once more assumed full control of the governments in the Southern states.

When President Rutherford B. Hayes withdrew the last troops from Louisiana, Florida, and South Carolina, home rule was fully restored to the South in 1877.

During the reconstruction period, three amendments, intended to define the new status of the Negroes, were added to the Constitution of the United States. The 13th, abolishing slavery; the 14th, guaranteeing full civil rights to the freedmen; and the 15th, granting them the right to vote. Reconstruction was not a purely political affair but was also economic and social.

The waste and destruction of the war had to be repaired. The Negro had to be taught to work as a free laborer, and to adjust himself to his new status in society. The old plantation system had to give way to one of small farms and tenants on shares.

Manufacturing, which during slavery times had made little headway in the South, now began to spread through the piedmont or foothills region of the southeast. Reconstruction was not confined merely to the South, because the North had an abundance of problems also caused by the Civil War.

A huge debt had been incurred and had to be paid; a currency issue of paper money had to be replaced on a gold basis; millions of men had to find new work either because they had been away in the war or because the increasing use of machinery, even though it was slow, had taken away many of their jobs.

Most of these problems continued beyond the reconstruction period. The events during and after the Civil War are too numerous to mention. But after many bloody battles the war finally ended in April 1865, leaving behind its unbelievably miserable suffering.

Now in the year of 1971, looking far beyond the grim horizon have the wounds and scars been permanently healed? Was the sacrifice worth the cause, or will history some day repeat itself? Who knows? Only the hands of time will tell. Even so, in this great country of ours more than 40,000 soldiers from North Carolina alone have lost their lives during the struggle for survival.

The Civil War has been written and entered into the pages of history as the bloodiest conflict ever to be recorded in the history of the United States of America. Four heartbreaking years when brother fought brother, brutally and savagely.

CHAPTER FIVE

The Change

Believe it or not, during those years of destruction between the North and the South, the war had little or no effect on the isolated village at East Lake where George Washington Creef, Jr. was busy growing up, chasing wild game down old Indian trails, also bringing home findings of Indian clay-pipe stems, clay peace pipes, arrowheads, tomahawks, and other rare pieces to decorate the mantle above the open fireplace.

The years swiftly passed. George was no longer a destructive little boy but a very useful constructive young man of eighteen. His father was by trade a boatbuilder, and Wash had taught his son the business. While George was growing up, he loved and respected his parents, helping them in every way possible.

He watched the fishing boats come and go, hoping that some day he could build one of his own, different from the ones he had seen. His father was aging, coming to the stage of life that everyone who lives must confront.

During George's few school years he learned the three R's in the rough, small one-room, one-teacher schoolhouse where he sat and whittled and carved his initials with his pocketknife on the homemade bench and desk. In the middle of the room stood a wood stove—its dented, rusty pipe went straight up past the rafters, and through the roof. During cold winter months the parents took turns in supplying wood for the stove. Over against the side of the wall stood a large wooden bucket filled with drinking water. A light-brown, coconut dipper bobbed up and down in it. At recess they all drank out of the same dipper.

Although young George Creef was a good boatbuilder, an excellent fisherman, and very ambitious, his education was limited and he was becoming restless as time passed. He knew that the outside world was in strange contrast to this isloated lonely little village as well as to the other nearby islands and beaches. All were set apart from one another and the mainland by poor transportation and communication.

It was December 11, 1874, and another day was ending. A huge, round, red ball of fire hung just above the treetops as Wash stepped from the dusty, worn, back steps which led from the porch to the ground.

Irregular dark-green treetops with wild shapes were silhouetted against the sky as strong northwest winds tossed them about. The black storm clouds making up in the north, and the icy chill in the air were signs of an early winter. On the back porch wood was piled high to be used for fuel in the open fireplace.

As usual, after supper the Creef family gathered in the living room. Popcorn burst into large snowy kernels in the pan Wash held over the bright yellow flame of the logs burning on the hearth. Crickets chirped in the warm dark corners of the chimney, and the winter winds roared through the trees outside.

Although young George loved and respected his home, he began discussing the possibility of venturing outside beyond his native village. However he quickly noticed a cloud of sorrow that hung in the hearts and minds of his parents.

Rebecca and Wash both knew that the time had long passed for this natural parting to take place. Their son had to establish a home for himself and find a mate. His mother's tears spoke for themselves. His father was old, and his heart ached and felt heavy at the thought of losing his son.

Quickly young George popped more corn over the burning embers. Moments later when he turned around, the tears were gone. His mother seemed to be in a more cheerful mood and had forced a smile to her troubled face. He promised not to mention it again, then quietly climbed the stairway to his room.

Before retiring for the night, Wash talked cautiously with Rebecca. Maybe their son would like to live on Roanoke Island, at Manteo, only about twelve miles away. With its wharfs at Wancheese and also at Manteo, at its feet the broad Pamlico Sound, full of the finest fish and oysters in the whole world, it probably held an excellent future for a young man in commercial fishing.

Icy winds brought snow flurries out of the north the next day from the low-hovering dark clouds that seemed to cover the sky just above the earth. By nightfall about three inches of crunchy snow covered the ground.

Wash lingered a while under the shelter, after he had finished feeding the restless half-starved livestock, then strolled out across the barnyard through the snow toward the kitchen where supper was waiting.

Steam rose from the yaupon spout and circled slowly about the room, curled drifted and mingled with the pleasant aroma of hot clabber biscuits. A large pan of snow cream was a treat for all the family after supper was over.

Later, sitting in a circle in the living room, watching the flames move lightly and quickly up from the burning logs in the fireplace as if they were licking the sides of the soot-covered chimney and enjoying the comfort from the heat along the clay-filled hearth, Rebecca launched the unforgettable subject of the Lost Colony.

The discussion went round and round. Young George remarked that they could have been killed by those savage Indians. Or, being there was no Croatan Sound at that time but only marsh, scattered storm-beaten scraggy trees, and low-spreading evergreen bushes on which delicious cranberries grew in abundance, they could have walked about three miles west from Roanoke Island to Croatan—which is better known today as Manns Harbor.

Rebecca nodded in agreement. "Yes, son, I don't suppose anyone will ever know just what really did happen to those stranded bewildered people. But someday Roanoke Island will be a strange historical island, and very prosperous." Rebecca sighed with relief as she glanced at the expression of understanding on her son's face. The approving smile that appeared helped to lighten the burden that continued to lie at anchor on his mother's and father's aching hearts.

During the next few years, young George stayed at home, helping with the family traditions. About every three or four months, the Creef family would sail to Roanoke Island by way of the Albemarle Sound, which was east. On reaching the island, they then sailed around the north end where they entered Roanoke Sound on the east side of the island. On and on the boat moved over the water until they reached Shallowbag Bay, which led to the docks at Manteo.

After several voyages, George was eager to return to this enchanting mystic island. This, of course, pleased his parents. Roanoke Island was not too far away and provided many more opportunities for betterment in their son's life which he so rightfully deserved.

It was a clear, starlit, warm night in June. A gentle, light breeze blew through the open bedroom window and across the bed as George lay watching the brilliant stars twinkle in the sky before he fell asleep.

Suddenly he awoke and gazed out of the open window into the silent blackness of the night. The Morning Star in the east told him that the dark hour just before dawn was close at hand. Today George would leave East Lake, to live on Roanoke Island and seek his fate—whether poverty or riches. The hour of decision had come at last.

It was October 25, 1881. The day broke cold, misty, and gray. Absence of the sun gave the day a gloomy appearance. Stillness filled the room as George climbed out of bed. Cautiously he moved about the room, to avoid disturbing the family at this early hour. Quietly he placed his few possessions close together in the narrow hallway just outside his bedroom door.

The four walls in the now unoccupied room stared and gave him an empty feeling. After pausing for a moment, he turned and moved noiselessly nearer the stairway. Then, hesitating no longer, he descended to the first floor.

To his surprise, the smell of fresh steaming yaupon was in the air. This had been a favorite drink among the natives for many centuries. Rebecca had been quietly busy preparing breakfast while her husband was outside feeding the stock. George walked across the room and sat down in his chair at the table near the window. He noticed that his father's footsteps were slowing.

He sat gazing out of the window at the barnyard and sipping the hot, rich-brown cup of yaupon, but felt no relief from a cold and lonely emptiness that began creeping along his throbbing veins. Certainly he did not want to leave his mother and father in their declining age. But he quickly assured them that he would return once each week, and stay with them overnight.

Taking a longer time than usual, he smiled as he finished his meal. Then he hurried up the stairway to move his few belongings down to the cart, where Nag stood waiting.

The dirt road they had to travel was no more than a winding trail which gradually led down from the house through the dense growth of underbrush and trees to the sound shore where

69

George Washington Creef's small valuable possession was moored.

The wind blew a light, steady breeze from the northwest. Gloom from the overcast began to clear. Blue skies were becoming visible through the broken clouds, and sunbeams cast warmth down on them while George finished loading the bobbing restless boat. When the small sail was unfurled and placed in position, the wind pressed steady against it and the boat slowly moved away from shore and headed out into broad Albemarle Sound. It was now nine o'clock in the morning. The sky was clear, the comforting warmth from the brilliant sunrays was strikingly different from the early icy air at daybreak. Nag moved inch by inch, munching on long blades of partly green grass along the shore. Rebecca and Wash sat in the cart, watching and waving as the small sailboat gradually disappeared from view.

George sailed into Shallowbag Bag at four o'clock in the afternoon, and soon was in sight of the Manteo dock at Roanoke Island. The natives were very friendly and helped him to get established on the island.

At this time Roanoke Island was mostly woods and little traveled. In the days that followed, George was active and dealing with reality. Generally speaking, geographically there was little or no change from his home at East Lake; but he now had to adjust himself to the surrounding circumstances which confronted him.

By trade, as mentioned before, he was a fine boatbuilder. But first he must work with someone, and save, in order to build the boat he had been visualizing for so long. A few days after his arrival George began working for a small railway on the northeast side of Roanoke Island, not far from Mother Vineyard where luscious wild grapes grew in abundance.

His desire to explore the island was keen and kept him occupied on weekends, searching in the ruins of the original Fort Raleigh and watching the fishing boats unload their catches at Wancheese.

Not long after George moved to Roanoke Island, he met and married the lovely Ann McCleese Baum. Ann lived in a clustered little fishing village called Baumtown, near the center of the island, between Manteo and Wancheese. At night George scarcely left home, and could be found with his family, chatting around the fireside and watching the live sparks from the burning logs in the fireplace dance up the chimney in gray curling smoke rings that brought back pleasant memories of his boyhood days.

Many Indian relics were found while he penetrated deep into the underbrush through the leaves and sticks. Rustling noises in the thick bushs, made by wild fowl and wild animals, were evidence of excellent hunting.

Here at Roanoke Island was the scene of a Civil War battleground, although it had not lasted for long. The Confederate States of America were formed in early February 1861, but North Carolina did not join them during the next three and a half months. The people went to the polls and voted down a proposal to call a special convention to consider secession from the Union. But Governor Ellis began acquiring military supplies to use for the Confederacy, if it actually came. North Carolina finally did secede from the Union and joined the Confederate States on May 20, which was about a month after President Lincoln called up troops to put down the rebellion by force.

I will only briefly sum up what actually happened on Roanoke Island during the Civil War.

At the outbreak of the war, the United States, or the North, wanted to control the inlets at Ocracoke, Hatteras, and Oregon Inlet; according to Lincoln, all were to be destroyed before the federal troops could use the inlets.

General Wise, a former Governor of Virginia, was ordered to take command of the defenses at Roanoke Island. He and his men marched from Richmond, Virginia. Along the way some of his colonels reported having a strange feeling about being sent to Roanoke Island, because they would be cut completely off from all communications with the rest of the army, and could eventually fall prey to the enemy. A feeling of mutiny began to spread among the troops at Petersburg, and as an example for the others, two soldiers were ordered shot. General Wise and his 5,000 men finally arrived at Roanoke Island, and immediately began to establish defenses there. Wise made his own headquarters on the beach at Nags Head.

Several battles were fought before the federal troops captured the forts and seized control of the inlets. Then the ships moved on across Pamlico Sound toward Roanoke Island. With the lower sounds and inlets in firm possession of the United States forces. Roanoke Island was and is still high on the north end, and low and marshy toward the south end.

Soon federal troops had landed on all sides, but only one brief battle was ever encountered. Confederates took up temporary positions beside the causeway, killing three men. General Wise was at Nags Head, where he was ill. Colonel Shaw, now in charge, knowing that his men were greatly outnumbered and would be slaughtered, surrendered Roanoke Island. A short time later, General Wise was captured at Nags Head by Colonel Hawkins.

CHAPTER SIX

Savonaro

It was a stormy night in late November. Friends gathered around the fire in the log cabins in the scattered neighborhood on Roanoke Island. The glare from the burning logs in the open fireplace on the rough walls of the living room was bright and warm while the whine of the wind outside and the patter of sleet on the windowpanes made strange sounds.

George Creef rose and moved his chair nearer to the fire, by the corner of the chimney. His face bronzed by the summer's sun, shone in the light. A sleek deerhound lay on the rug on the floor, exposed to the light from the blaze, while Ann occupied an armchair that looked as ancient as the hills.

More chips and small branches were thrown on the coals as they sat watching the blaze rise and fall, the red glow get pale, and the reddish embers darken while the shadows grew dim and died. Soon a lull followed. George went to the door and looked out. The storm had passed. Stars shone in the open spaces between the scattered black clouds that slowly drifted across the sky.

The wind blew an icy mist from the pines and wet his face as he continued to stand in the doorway and gazed up at the sky. The chill of winter was in the air. Trees in the forest looked bare and desolate against the stormy unsettled clearing in the firmament.

The flame inside the clear glass globe of the lamp flickered from the motion of the wind as George closed the door. Moments later, short footsteps soon brought them to their bedside and eventually stopped them off in dreamland—maybe to engage on some lofty venture.

The next day broke clear and cold, the wind blew strong from the northwest. After breakfast George picked up his small tin bucket partly filled with grub, bid his family good-by for the day, and started walking hurriedly toward the dock at Shallowbag Bay where his fishing boat lay waiting to take him out to the fishing grounds in Pamlico Sound. There many different kinds of fish could be caught, such as roe shad, speckled trout, blues, spots, mullets, and many other varieties of the best eating fish in the world.

During certain times of the year enormous numbers of these fish came in from the ocean through the inlets into the Pamlico Sound, south of Roanoke Island, making commercial fishing very profitable.

As George walked around the bend near the dock he smiled at the sight of his small but seaworthy sailboat as she swung slowly from side to side at her mooring. Low, ill-shaped, scraggy pines and deep-green water bushes swayed in the wind. Blackbirds, perched on tall marsh sage grass, bobbed up and down while they sang their morning song. Sheets of thin ice, that had formed the night before on the surface of the water in Shallowbag Bay, made crackling sounds against the sides of the boat as George sailed toward the open waters of Pamlico Sound.

Today, as on many other winter days, George watched the marsh grass bristle like small peaks from patches of webbed ice along this lonely route. Wild ducks and geese flew low overhead practically unnoticed.

About two hours later, as George sailed away from the southernmost tip of Roanoke Island, or Wancheese shores, he noticed that the tide was far below normal. This and many other signs of nature, known only to the natives of this enchanted land, gave him the feeling of a successful day.

Surely his hunch was right. After many sets his nets were full of rod shad and blues, and his small boat was loaded to capacity. The shallowness in some parts of the sounds and bays which surrounded Roanoke Island certainly was a condition that no one could afford to overlook when the keel was laid to build a boat to be used successfully in these shallow waters. On the way in, the center board dragged bottom several times before George reached the fish house at the dock in Manteo, along the shoreline of Shallowbag Bay.

While sorting out his day's catch at the wharf, George put aside a dozen pan mullets to take home for supper. By the time he finished, the sun was sinking behind the storm clouds that had formed late in the afternoon just above the tree tops as George left on foot for home.

Although she had been busy with the house chores, it had been a long and lonesome day for Ann. From the kitchen window, she now kept a continual watch on the path while she was fixing supper. A few moments passed, twilight began to fade, and soon George Creef strolled up the path that led to the back of the house.

While the mullets fried in the deep cast-iron spider on the stove over the wood fire, clabber biscuits browned in the oven, and yaupon slowly perked on the back of the stove. George sat on a low stool in the corner behind the stove, absorbing the heat as the conversation began to intensify.

When supper was over, and they were enjoying the warmth from the burning logs in the fireplace in the drab little living room, happenings of the day were discussed by both. Then George began to talk about the kind of materials he needed to build a large, almost flat V-bottom boat that was badly needed for the betterment of all here in this almost isolated part of the world.

From time to time he made notes on the most important facts about the depth of the waters in the four sounds which surrounded Roanoke Island, the location of the best fishing grounds, the best oyster beds, and the kind of boat that would best serve the purpose for all-around needs a boat that would be spacious enough to successfully work these commercial opportunities, and also be navigable in most of the shallow places.

But where was he to get the long thick boards, light enough to build a boat of this type in order that she might have a shallow draft? In deep thought, George gazed into the open fire from the cracking logs as unbridled and noiseless flames rose high, licked the sides of the chimney, and pieces of soot fell on the hearth. He searched for an answer as he sipped a cup of hot yaupon before retiring for the night.

During the next few years he worked and saved all the money possible, with the excellent cooperation of his wife. Then one day, at Shallowbag Bay while he leisurely stood on the dock that led on up toward Mother Vineyard, George suddenly decided to build a small railway just large enough to pull and repair active fishing boats.

Through his own efforts, and also with the help of others, he soon acquired about an acre of land around the curve in the

75

shoreline in Manteo, not far from the dock on Shallowbag Bay. A thicket of low, windblown oaks and jagged pines stood protruding out over the water's edge along the shore. Thick clusters of rich, dark-green water bushes also grew nearby.

The land was cleared with the help of former Negro slaves—now freed by the Civil War and left on Roanoke Island—who were hired and paid the same wages as anyone else. After several weeks, piling was put into place, then skids, and a large cradle was made ready. Another step forward toward George Washington Creef's dream to better serve mankind.

At this time, before the turn of the twentieth century, there was no machinery known, at least not to the natives on the island, that could be used to pull the boats up out of the water and on a railway. George rigged up a large winch, with a long wire cable wound several times around it. His favorite old white horse, named Old Jack, was used along with the cable and winch to take the place of machinery that was so badly needed but not available to pull the boats out of the water.

After the boats were repaired, Old Jack was used to keep the cable taut, while the boats slowly slid down the railway and back into the water. This system worked very well. Many fishing boats in need of repair came up the narrow rippling Shallowbag Bay, which flowed toward the broad Roanoke and Albemarle sounds.

On November 19, 1887, the wind shifted and blew from the northeast with terrific force. It was before midnight. The wind howled and wailed outside, while a sticky warmth filled the air inside the house. Worn stools and high-backed rocking chairs rested against the wall in the drab corners of the unfinished room in the Creef home.

Suddenly their informal conversation about the storm ceased. George rose from his chair and slowly walked across the room to the window. He cupped his face in his hands and expressed a desire to observe the velocity of the storm through complete darkness.

Many times he had heard the roaring desolate sounds made by the force of the icy wind, and each time he welcomed it as a total stranger. Numerous thoughts wandered through his mind as he again sat before the fireplace, moving his fingers through his thinning hair, smoking his pipe in silence, and listening to the rain beating down with such driving force that the roof leaked in many places.

Meanwhile an able four-masted sailing schooner, loaded with virgin heart and Georgia pine, was battling high winds and monstrous waves off the dangerous North Carolina coastline. On November 17, 1887, the schooner *Savonaro* had been completely loaded with her cargo after several difficult days of hard labor. She now lay in a beautiful safe harbor, secured to the dock by her huge hawsers, sixteen miles from the broad Atlantic Ocean.

The harbor at Savannah, Georgia, was in all its glory. Captain Gilmo was strolling around this colonial city of Savannah, admiring its beauty and leisurely moving down the wide tree-lined streets which were intersected at regular intervals by small parks and squares. Originally the squares had been intended as points of defense against Indian and Spanish attacks.

The scent of blossoms of gardenias, camellias, and azaleas perfumed the night air. Palmettos, magnolias, and great old live oak trees hung with Spanish moss, gave Savannah the name Forest City.

Monuments to the Revolutionary and Confederate heroes stood in many of the exciting lovely parks. Old brick colonial houses with high stoops, iron railings, and half-hidden moss-covered gardens added to the beauty and leisurely charm of this seaport town of Savannah, Georgia. Captain Gilmo suddenly stopped and drew a long deep breath of the clean fresh air brought by a light breeze that blew from the west across the deep, quiet Savannah River.

Everything seemed so peaceful. He turned and walked toward the well-kept wharfs, where the faithful schooner *Savonaro* lay at ease. How wonderful it was. The night was young. The lights from the oil-fed street lamps bobbed slowly up and down as he passed them.

Savannah was the oldest and largest city in Georgia. The Savannah River was formed by junction of the Tugaloo and Seneca rivers. The Savannah River is four hundred and fifty miles long, and flows into the Atlantic Ocean. The city of Savannah is built on a flat sandy bluff forty feet high. It is beautifully laid out with wide streets and many squares, most of which are adorned by magnolias, live oaks, and other stately trees.

Georgia was well known all over the world for its famous virgin long-leaf pine forest. Some trees were of giant size, with trunks rising upwards to two hundred feet, and were from seven to nearly twelve feet in diameter. The lumber from the large tall trees out of the huge dark forest was used in the manufacture of furniture, carvings, and shipbuilding. About two blocks away from the dock, as he drew near his schooner, Captain Gilmo heard music and then singing and laughter.

Puffing on his pipe while he strolled across the cobblestone street toward the dock, memories of street dances back home, when he was a boy, suddenly lived again. This was their last night at Savannah. Tomorrow, before dawn, they would sail.

On a small wooden box sat a teen-age boy named Tom. Between his knees he held an old metal washboard, and in each hand a seasoned hickory stick with which he kept time with the king of banjo picking—John Snowy. Jim was playing the harmonica and accordion, while Sam joined in with his base guitar that was really talking.

Everyone was dancing, singing, swinging, and swaying. Some old-timers were smiling from ear to ear, stamping and patting their knees with their open palms. Fun and laughter for all. At last, near midnight, it was time to say farewell. Many wished Captain Gilmo and his crew of nine the best of luck, and departed for home.

A few minutes later the captain and crew were in their bunks, fast asleep. Steve was left alone on deck, to stand watch from midnight until 4 A.M. It was lonely. A lull had fallen over the harbor, as if time stood still. Gulls sat on pilings with their heads low and slept with bills resting on their craws.

During the night the wind moved gently from the west, around to the south, and now a soft breeze blew over the water. The Savannah River was virtually calm and quiet, not a sound from the tiny ripples. The moon looked down on the sleeping world, brightly shimmering and dancing on the little ripples of the great waterway that led to the broad Atlantic Ocean. Only the striking chimes from a faraway town clock broke the dead silence of the night. Wharf rats ran quietly to and fro on the large hemp hawser.

At 4 A.M. Steve called the skipper and the crew, then went cautiously down the narrow steep steps to the galley below deck and made a large pot of fresh coffee. Soon all were up. Then, breakfast over, orders were given to unfurl the sails. At daybreak the wind had grown stronger, and now it blew a steady brisk breeze against the mainsail. Orders were given for their departure, and slowly the schooner *Savonaro* moved away from the dock and on down the beautiful Savannah River toward the sea.

Bill, the cook, was busy preparing dinner in the galley. The smell of food from below mingled with the steam from the coffeepot where it stood perking on the back of the stove. Soon the dinnerbell rang. Over the brown biscuits, roast beef, potatoes and gravy, their stay at Savannah was thoroughly discussed among themselves and treasured in their hearts.

About three hours later, the schooner sailed out of the river and Captain Gilmo steered his ship for the open sea. Before him and his crew lay the vast Atlantic Ocean. The wind blew strong; the sails were full; all was well. Sparkling spray breaking on the sides near the bow made an unforgettable picture as the sun rose higher in the sky. A pleasure for Captain Gilmo and his crew to sail such a well-built, four masted schooner, with so many thousands of miles and so many successful voyages to her credit.

Although the *Savonaro* had encountered many fierce storms, she had always been able to ride them out. She was respected by every seafarer. Only once in the past fourteen years her crew had been forced to cast part of her cargo into the sea, during a terrible storm in the mid-Atlantic, to lighten the vessel while she struggled to survive.

Some of the crew were now watching and admiring how smoothly the vessel was gliding along under full sail. Her main spreading white sails set full to catch the force of the wind, her jib, or triangular sail, projecting ahead of the foremast; and her topsail, made a marvelous picture against the clear blue sky.

On and on she sailed up the North Carolina Coast. Soon they would be abreast of Diamond Shoals. For many centuries, captains and seamen alike have dreaded these dangerous shoals off Cape Hatteras, which are about five miles from land. Some refer to them as treacherous and shifting; but some of the old-timers who had lived at Cape Hatteras, and the Outer-Banks pilots who have known these shoals for many hundred years, will tell you the shoals are not a continuous bulk but rather a series of three different or separate shoals, with channels between them, and deep enough so that ships can pass through them in favorable weather—provided they know where the channels really are. But how many seamen would want to chance this risk?

The night watch on the *Savonaro* took his post just before dusk faded and darkness closed in. In a few hours she would be nearing the dangerous shoals. The helmsman stood beside the sturdy oaken wheel, and continued to guide her on her course. The crew was at ease, some were still talking about the friendly and generous entertainment of the people back at the famous Savannah Harbor. The first mate strolled fore and aft to make sure that everything was secure for the night.

Suddenly the sky became dark and seemed very close, the air was cold, salt spray collected on the mate's coat. The vessel was now passing Cape Lookout Lightship, which rolled and pitched at anchor, warning the ships of the long and large shoals off Cape Lookout, although they were not considered as dangerous as the nest of shoals which can be seen on a stormy day by standing on Cape Point at Hatteras and watching two oceans come together in wild and violent anger. At Cape Point the northbound warm Gulf Stream and the cold currents coming down from the Arctic run head-on together, tossing their spray upward in the air for several feet, dropping sea shells, sand, and fish at the point where these two great strong currents meet. This is what is supposed to have formed the dreaded Diamond Shoals —shifting sandbars, often pushing seaward and causing such a hazard for the passing ships at sea, known to all seafaring men as the Graveyard of the Atlantic. Actually they extend along the whole North Carolina coast.

Hundreds of wrecked vessels, all a total loss, are buried there: the skeletons of countless ships, some covered by sand, some by water, and some bare-ribbed, parts known only to the men who went down into eternity with them.

The schooner *Savonaro* sailed on. Captain Gilmo was calm, though the night grew extremely dark and gloomy and he seemed to sense or became aware of something nearby. He called his crew together and gave the command to stand by for further orders. There was a tense feeling among them as the men stood waiting.

Within a few minutes, a howling, roaring northeast gale was whipping and piling the sea up high. The storm struck with great fury. Heavy rain came down with such force that it was almost three inches deep on the main deck, but it swiftly ran off on each side through the oval openings along the sides of the ship's railing.

Captain Gilmo gave orders to take in the topsail and the jib. The schooner was very seaworthy. She had weathered many roaring typhoons in the Sea of Japan and in the China Sea. The *Savonaro* had defied previous storms of the North Atlantic, but this time her cargo was very heavy and hard to handle. Every available space was loaded with the famous long-leaf heart pine from the huge dense Georgia forests.

Many records show that these storms at sea seem to come from nowhere and strike like a savage, monstrous beast. The harsh realities of the untamed sea have transformed many men into hard-driving, straightforward, not-so-easy-going human beings. This kind of experience would harden even the best men, bring them down to reality and rudely show them the tougher side of life.

Ever since ships have been sailing the mighty oceans, man has found out early that the challenge of the open sea was far beyond the capacity of human beings. Man must regard nature with the deepest respect, for he so often finds himself powerless against it.

The only seven-masted schooner ever to be built in the world, the *Thomas W. Larson,* was wrecked in a storm where strong winds and heavy seas suddenly prevailed without warning off the coast of Long Island, New York. But ships must sail all over the world in order to keep up trade with other nations, regardless of the sacrifice.

Captain Gilmo appeared worried as the storm grew in strength. Courage, strength, and faith was needed to fight on in these troubled waters. The skipper stood as if frozen to the helm, looking for the beacon in the Cape Hatteras Lighthouse at Buxton, North Carolina. It towered two hundred and eight feet above sea level; the tallest lighthouse on the American coastline, and the first to be built here in 1802. It was almost destroyed during the Civil War, with the North and the South blaming each other for the damage. The present structure was built in 1870, and towers almost twice the height of the original one. When the atmosphere is clear, the beacon is visible for a distance of at least

81

twenty miles at sea. Its purpose is to warn ships of the dangerous Diamond Shoals, the treacherous waters of the Atlantic along the North Carolina coast.

Also in the year of 1824, a three hundred and twenty-ton lightship constructed in New York was anchored off Cape Hatteras at the tip of the outer Diamond Shoals, to warn all passing ships away from these turbulent seas that constantly roamed these shoals and have claimed over six hundred ships and thousands of poor troubled souls.

Then, for nearly three years, the lightship was under the command of Captain Holden, who with his family and crew lived aboard the vessel anchored near the most dangerous spot along the North Carolina coast. Later, while a storm raged, her anchor cable parted under the pounding of the heavy seas, and the lightship drifted toward the shoals. Some hours later, after a heavy beating and the loss of her sails and several lives, she was sighted by local residents early the next morning, hard aground abreast of old Whalebone Inlet, and soon all were helped safely ashore. For many years afterward there was no lightship, and no more warning light bobbed up and down from the motion of the ship on the outer edge of the dreaded shoals.

Tonight Captain Gilmo took every necessary precaution, and the crew helped in every way possible. The storm bore down on the struggling, fighting ship. After several attempts, the first mate made his way to the helm where the skipper now wrestled with the wheel.

Not a word was spoken as he tried to relieve the weary and exhausted man, but Captain Gilmo refused to budge. Strong and ugly gusts of wind up to hundred and twenty miles an hour, ripped with great force into the mainsail like the goring horns of an angry bull. Gigantic waves bore down on the vessel like a ferocious beast devouring its prey. Up came her nose, and she trembled and groaned under the terrific pounding.

Then thunderous, high-foaming waves hit the schooner on her starboard side. The rudder broke loose, leaving her completely out of control. She was now at the mercy of violent wind and angry waves. Gusts of wind continued to roar and moan as the mast made creaking sounds and began to split. In moments, the mast was twisted into splinters and stripped of its sails.

82

All rockets, flares, and coston signals were used up. Captain Gilmo stared hopelessly into the darkness. Visibility was down to zero. He no longer scanned the horizon for the sight of the Cape Hatteras Lighthouse beacon, but fought desperately for survival. The icy salt spray that swept across his face had the smell of death as it continued to fill the air.

The skipper uttered a prayer: "God! Take me if it be thy will, but please save my men and my ship." As he looked up, this powerful black ghost was hovering overhead. His ship was fighting for her very life, but was as helpless as an autumn leaf in a hurricane gale. Some of the crew were clinging to the side of the broken and battered railing when she neared the outer bar off the coast of lower Nags Head, North Carolina. Her beam split, and many of her ribs cracked as the heavy waves and merciless wind pounded her when she struck the sandbar. Soon the timbers began to loosen, and she rapidly went to pieces.

Captain Gilmo and crew were buried in this vast watery grave that has claimed so many poor, tortured human souls—of which there will be no end so long as men sail these untamed seven seas around the world.

At daybreak, all that remained of the schooner *Savonaro* were a few of her timbers. Her cargo of virgin pine was scattered for miles along the beach.

CHAPTER SEVEN

Astounded

The storm passed, taking its toll. Many ships and many lives had been lost during storms at sea, but few accurate records had been kept. In some instances no records at all were made during the earlier years, or in the distant past.

George Creef rose the next morning before daybreak, the hour of gray gloom and then the lighting of dawn. The weather had made a marvelous recovery from the previous night. He opened his eyes wide as he gazed at the glorious golden shafts of sunlight through the oak and pine forest that overlooked the east side of Roanoke Island. The sun had risen high enough to tip the cedar groves near the shoreline with a long brilliant slant on Shallowbag Bay.

The west side of this mysterious historical island lay still and asleep. Dark-green, ghostly shadows, merged into the early morning mist as the sun rose higher. George fed his hungry dogs while Ann was fixing breakfast.

Today the wind was calm. Rough, angry waves subsided as usual after such a terrible northeast storm. The sun looked sleepy, and the wind was low while the natives prepared to cross Roanoke Sound in their small sailboats. They would then walk from the sound shore and across the beach, about one mile to the surf, in search of treasure. This was the usual custom after a terrific storm. Roanoke Sound lies to the east of Roanoke Island, and separates the island from the beach.

Soon George went hurriedly down the rough dusty road to the dock at Shallowbag Bay, only a short distance away from his home, then sailed his small boat out of the bay and into Roanoke Sound. With hardly enough wind to sail, he used his oars to help the boat through the clear blue water in order to reach the beach on the other side of the sound.

After pulling the bow of the boat up on shore, George quickly walked through the low ill-shaped pines. He watched a drove of wild ponies feeding on rich, deep-green, water bushes scattered on the beach along the way to the surf.

Standing atop a small sand dune, not far from the edge of the surf, George was suddenly astonished by the scene before him, For many years he had searched along the surf for treasures from the sea, but now he could hardly believe his own eyes.

The beach was strewn with heart pine squared logs. Some were at least forty feet long. Strange, deep reasoning began to circulate through his mind. Was this a dream, or were these virgin heart-pine logs real?

He found himself running through the soft sand to touch the logs to make sure. Beside one of the logs a man lay face down, mumbling and begging for help. Quickly George raised the wounded man and propped him up against the log. On the man's bare chest there were many cuts and bruises. On his left arm the words S T E V E was plainly tatooed in blue ink.

George gave him all the assistance possible, and soon Steve began to talk. After telling George about his horrible experience, the screaming, the dying, the gigantic waves and the storm of the night before, Steve suddenly passed into eternity. Soon afterward he was buried on the beach along the sand dunes, where he can still hear the cries of the departed poor souls while the sea refuses to give up its dead.

A lifesaving station, one of several established on the Outer Banks, at this particular time of the year was closed and inactive. The keeper was home on Roanoke Island, miles away across the Roanoke Sound. Congress had failed to provide enough money for operating the station on a full-time basis.

George Washington Creef's heart was filled with sorrow because these poor tortured souls had paid the price with their lives. With great effort he struggled to awaken to the reality of the moments, while a dark overcast seem to cause a heavy slumber that sailed the channel of his mind.

Some time had passed, George stood scanning and glancing slowly up and down the beach, along the surf. He noticed scattered pieces of a wrecked schooner. After severe storms, sometimes parts of ships that had sunk many decades ago could be seen and salvaged by the natives.

Scores of souvenirs had been found over a period of time— odd-shaped jugs, brass winches, pilot wheels, navigation instruments, even gold Spanish and Mexican coins. The southerly winds that blow during the summer months allow the sea to build up the beach, piling the sand high. In some places, partly covered sea shells and pebbles of many colors and sizes were waiting along the surf to give pleasure to some little boys and girls with their sand buckets, hoping to be taken back to their homes—maybe to some faraway place to spread around beautiful flowerbeds in memory of their lovely vacation at the seashore.

About three hundred feet of the beach, from the surf, had been washed away and the sand dunes leveled by the monstrous storm that had passed the night before and left so much unrest, strife, death, and destruction.

Large, fleecy white clouds began to move across the peaceful light-blue sky as George stood gazing at so many valuable pieces of timber that had been washed up high on the beach. Low waves rolled slowly toward the shore, breaking gently on the sand; and sea gulls sailed a few feet high overhead, screeching their shrill cries in their own language. Sea chickens, in search of sand fleas which they used for food, ran swiftly to and fro with the waves that constantly washed the shore.

The sun was extremely bright; it was a wonderful late fall day. Wild ponies could be seen pawing holes in the sand, searching for fresh water to drink. Nature had taught them the ways of survival many many years ago after they had been ship-wrecked along the North Carolina coast while being shipped from their native home in Arabia to many parts of the world for breeding purposes. Now they roamed the beaches of the Outer Banks in droves; many were stunted in their growth by being poorly fed.

George Creef gazed calmly at the vast space of the blue Atlantic. He could imagine the horrors that had befallen the ill-fated schooner and all aboard her the night before. History was once more taking its place among the pages of time, nothing could be changed. George took one more look at the valuable timber scattered along this almost uninhabited barren sandy beach, then turned and walked away toward the sound shore where his small sailboat waited to take him back to Roanoke Island. Uncertain reasoning carefully explored his thoughts as they sprang up in his mind while he moved along on foot at a moderate pace through the soft sand.

It was then about four o'clock in the afternoon. George glanced casually at a drove of wild ponies feeding on dark-green clumps of low-water bushes that grew in the lowest moist places on the beach. He noticed that some of the ponies had heavy bodies and strong necks and shoulders, although their legs were rather short. Some were feeding on the scattered head-high bushes and beach grass, also the sea oats which grew wild about three or four feet tall and provided food for them.

Taking a longer time than usual, George approached them carefully. But this made no difference; they threw their heads up high and snorted and whinnied while they quickly ran away, led by a handsome sorrel stud. George was now about halfway across the beach, from the surf to the sound side. He began to think about the way he had helped each year with the round-up of the ponies, which then were loaded on small flat barges and towed by sailboats to the far-away mainland and auctioned off to the highest bidder. Many of these horses were used on farms in Currituck County. It was a regular money business for the natives along the Outer Banks.

Suddenly, he had an idea that these wild ponies were strong enough to pull this valuable timber across the sandy beach to the Roanoke Sound side as they raced through the low underbrush.

When he reached the sound shore, George felt tired and exhausted. Before leaving the shore for home, he tried desperately not to think about the terrible disaster that was so heavy on his mind. He recalled other vessels that had been lost on the dangerous shoals off the treacherous coast of North Carolina, such as the *Enterprize*, the *Thomas A. Blount*, and the *Harvest*. During the Civil War, from 1861 to 1865, the peerless *Mohican* loaded with stores, the *Governor* carrying 6,000 marines, and the *Isaac Smith*, all had fallen prey to the shoal-infested sea off Cape Hatteras. The *Thames*, that grounded and burned off Cape Hatteras in April 1869; *Templar* and *Kensington*, in a collision off Diamond Shoals, had been a total loss in 1871; the *Metropolis*, that was destroyed off Currituck Beach in 1878; the *Dulcimer*, loaded with sugar, wrecked off Cape Hatteras in 1883. Also the *Ephraim Williams*, four hundred and ninety-one tons, loaded with lumber from Savannah, Georgia, and lost off Frying Pan Shoals in December 1884. All a total loss. And there were many more almost too numerous to mention.

George Creef's spirits were low; he was saddened by the thoughts that ran through his weary mind. He remembered the *Huron*, off Nags Head, in November 1877, when one hundred and three were drowned. Even today, beneath the blue ocean water a few feet away from the beach on the sandbar. the rusted. broken, and twisted government boat is still visible. Little or no relief did George find in thinking of these horrible sea disasters, and the thousands of poor tortured souls who went down to their watery grave.

George pushed the little sailboat away from shore, raised the sail, and started for home.

The great stretch of fascinating ocean front which extends from Georgetown, South Carolina, to Topsail Inlet on the North Carolina coast is the unmarked graveyard of many, many ships that once sailed the seas. Some of them fought in the Civil War for the Confederacy, the bloody war between the states. By following on a map, you will see the peculiar formation—an amazing number of hidden sandbars, inlets for miles and miles, sounds, inland waterways, rivers, and juniper swamps. The North Carolina coastline is very unusual in a structural and geographical way. The trade winds, the ocean currents and mountainous waves man will never change though locked in a battle for survival with this mad devourer. Many mysteries that had happened along the North Carolina coast remain stubbornly unsolved after many centuries, as previously mentioned, but will be remembered.

In 1889, on September 19, another unforgettable storm struck with terrific force on Ocrakoke Island, leaving many homeless. Houses were either blown to pieces, or the heavy seas washed them away. After the storm passed, most of the natives searched for a few belongings. Then they left in small boats, crossed Pamlico Sound and settled on Roanoke Island. This increased the population, because at that time only about twelve or fifteen families were living on the island at Manteo.

Today some of the drab, moss-dotted, one-room shacks which the families from Ocrakoke built and had lived in still stand at Manteo. Surely a memory of the past to a few of the older natives of the island, where owls sat on limbs on the darkest nights near the edge of the forest and made hair-raising noises;

and where savage Indians once crept around as noiselessly as snowflakes on a quiet winter night. Here the cold moon rose and shone on the white sand and tall banks along Roanoke Sound, where Mother Vineyard, over three hundred years old, still bears delicious grapes in abundance.

Treasure of the wild, on this island of mystery and charm.

During the next few days some of the natives admired the virgin timber lying on the beach, went on their way to look for washed-up treasures from the ocean depths. Others knew there was no possible way to move the timber. And some, using a cross-cut saw, cut it into blocks for firewood. But not George Creef. This timber must be salvaged, sent to a sawmill, and cut into boards to be used for building the boat he had dreamed about But how? The nearest sawmill was about forty-four miles away along the Pasquotank River, at the entrance to the harbor at Elizabeth City, North Carolina.

With little or no transportation available, more than ever before George Creef now realized just how important better transportation and communication were needed in this part of the state, where the Outer Banks and their neighboring nearby islands were practically isolated.

This great historical part of our nation, the very birth of our nation, was all but forgotten. The hardships which the early settlers such as The Lost Colony had endured, must rise from the pages of history and take the proper place among our courageous forefathers who had sacrificed so much for the beginning of our great country.

Once more George plowed along through the soft sand and over the scattered grass-studded little sand dunes, thinking that after all those heart-pine squared logs were not so heavy, nothing like the logs before the sap sides were cut off. Could he use Old Jack, that had been so faithful at the railway, to drag the timber across the beach to the sound? Oh, no! Old Jack was getting too old, and was trained for his job at the railway where he must stay.

Only one thought now ran through his mind as he sailed across the sound for home. Later he entered Shallowbag Bay, and secured his boat for the night. The sun was just above the treetops, sinking slowly behind them. It blazed brightly on the dusty road that led from the dock to his home a short distance away, where his wife and children anxiously awaited his return.

Hot biscuits, brown gravy, and deer meat were passed around the supper table, and Ann was busy pouring more freshly perked coffee into large thick coffee mugs. No questions were asked, but Ann saw the worried look on George's tired face.

Soon the delicious meal was over, and the family gathered near the fire in the living room. All were eager to hear about the findings along the surf. The light from the flames of the burning oak logs in the open fireplace now plainly reflected the strain of the day's happenings in his eyes. George hardly knew where to start, but he was aware of the silence that now filled the drab little room as he began to unravel the eventful happenings he had encountered during the day.

The family appeared too deeply moved to speak, as if everyone was listening to a description of a thrilling dream. Quiet gripped the room, except for the cracking and popping noises made by the logs burning in the fireplace. Then a few questions slowly came forth, and a lengthy discussion followed. But some questions were left unanswered.

George rose from his chair as the clock on the mantle chimed twelve o'clock, strolled across the room, opened the front door, and stepped out on the short narrow porch to direct his attention on the weather.

A friendly, steady breeze blew from the west. The long arms of moss, hanging artfully from the limbs on the old tree that grew near the corner of the house, waved back and forth as George gazed up at the sky. The atmosphere was clear, the air was sharp. A neighbor's dog barked at some unknown creature. The stars twinkled brightly in the firmament, casting a ray of starlight on the earth. Soon he returned to the warm room, and a few moments later climbed the rickety old stairs and went to the bedroom, where he laid his pipe on the edge of the window sill before dropping off to sleep.

George slept longer than usual the next morning. Ann moved quietly about the kitchen until breakfast was ready, because she knew her hard-working husband had been under a great physical and mental strain from the rare experiences of the day before. Finally George was aroused from sleep by the smell of yaupon steaming on the wood stove, and mingling with it was the aroma of the salt herrings frying in the pan in the kitchen beneath his bedroom.

Although it was early in the day, the sun was a few hours high in the sky. George was in no hurry. He sat on the side of his bed, pondering over his problems, trying to map out a course of what he intended to do about the timber.

Through the small window a ray of sunlight from the clear blue sky cast a beam on the floor. Moments later George broke a thin layer of ice on the water in the bucket that stood on a short wooden bench on the back porch, and washed his face.

Hot embers rose up the clay chimney from the blazing fire in the fireplace, while outside the bright sun smiled down on this quiet chilled little village. George walked down the dirt road toward the dock, to the only means of transportation that he had.

For the benefit of those who have not had the pleasure of sailing one of those earlier constructed small sailboats: George Creef had one of the finest that could be built on the island during that early age. His boat was eighteen feet in length, and seven feet in width. In the center, a slot one and a half inches wide and two feet long was cut through the bottom. A watertight frame was built around it, about eighteen inches high inside the boat. At the forward end of the slot, a board placed on its edge was fastened at the forward end with a small bolt dropped through the slot and left swinging through the bottom of the boat into the water.

The aft end of the centerboard was left free, with a short piece of window-sash cord fastened to it so it could be pulled up or down while the boat was moving through the water, powered only by a small sail from its mast. This was used to help control and guide the boat, more like a fish fin serving the same purpose.

Boats of this type were built from thin lumber; sometimes juniper was used. Usually they had a flat bottom, because in most places the water was shallow near the shore, and sometimes also further out from the shore. They were very convenient, the only means or source of transportation and communication with others in the Outer Banks and on the mainland.

When it was calm, and there was not enough wind to sail, a set of oars and oar locks were always carried in the boat to row the hull through the water.

91

On this day, members of the Creef family were more than delighted when George agreed to take them with him in his proud little sailboat to see the valuable timber that was still scattered about the beach along the surf.

Soon they were looking up and down the beach at the unbelievable sight, while George stood deep in thought. Suddenly he blurted out the idea of catching two of the strong, able-bodied wild ponies and using them to drag the timber with chains across the beach to the sound side. Once the squared timber was in the sound water and out deep enough to float, Wash could fasten the logs together with chains and dogs and form a raft, and then pull them by sailboat across the Roanoke and Albermarle sounds. Then he could sail past Camden Point and out of North River, which poured into the reddish-brown waters of the Pasquotank River that leads to Elizabeth City, North Carolina. This route is about forty-four miles by sailboat in normal weather.

At this time, during the late 1800s, the Outer Banks were very thinly populated; only small scattered groups dotted the beaches. There were only seven tiny lifesaving stations, placed miles apart and poorly kept on a part-time basis, mostly by volunteers, in times of trouble. Only a house here and there could be seen up in the Nags Head woods section on the sound side.

In 1875, at Currituck Beach, a red-brick lighthouse one hundred and fifty feet high was constructed. At Kitty Hawk, a small United States Weather Bureau Station was built in 1875, and operated until 1904. Also at Kitty Hawk, in 1878 Captain Bill Tate's wife Sophia established the first Post Office, which at that time was in Currituck County.

During the last part of the nineteenth century some of the natives began to expand and search for better ways of living, although about 90 percent of them were satisfied with the sandy beaches, high irregular hills covered mostly with thick growths of scraggy long-leaf pine, low dark-green live oaks, and scattered holly. These beautiful forest-covered hills are in some places, separated by swamps and sandy valleys. At Duck, which is located just north of Kitty Hawk, may be seen some of these lovely tree-covered sand hills. A small fishing village on the Currituck Sound side of the beach, with a population of about sixty people, made up the main part of Duck Village.

So much has already been written about these small scattered and isolated villages along the Outer Banks, that I shall endeavor not to make this much-discussed subject boring and mention only enough to enlighten the readers on a situation with which the natives were struggling in this all but forgotten portion of North Carolina, so far as transportation and communication were concerned.

George Washington Creef knew about this situation; and more than anyone else, viewed it with a definite purpose in mind.

The next day, with the help of George Moore and Mose Midgette, two men who worked with George at the railway on Roanoke Island along the quiet shores on Shallowbag Bay, he singled out two strong sorrel mares from the herd of wild ponies on the beach. Then the mares were rushed and forced into the sound, where they were captured and roped.

After a day or two they became easier to handle. At first the ponies were very wild, afraid, and distrustful. But this soon began to change as they wore themselves down, after being waded out deep in the mud and water all day in order to get them to be more relaxed. From experience George knew that mares were much easier to break and work than studs. Ninety-nine studs out of a hundred were mean and hard to handle even after they had been broken in.

On the third day after the mares were captured, while the stars shone brightly overhead just before dawn, the first heart-pine timber began to move across the beach and toward the sound shore. With hardly any physical strain at all on the ponies, side by side this pair of mares dragged log after log until the work was finished.

Meanwhile, back on the island, gossip and voices ran high. George Creef must be losing his mind. But this kind of chatter went unnoticed by him. His mind was too busy with plans to build a boat out of this light heart-pine.

This boat, as mentioned before, must be light as possible in order to sail in the shallow sounds around the island; it also must be large enough to be successfully used for all commercial fishing, and carry freight along with passengers and mail.

CHAPTER EIGHT

Uncertain Journey

Dare County was now only eight years old. It was formed in 1870 from parts of three other counties—Hyde, Tyrrell, and Currituck. All the Outer Banks, from Hatteras Inlet going north, to Caffeys Inlet, including Roanoke Island, Nags Head, and Collington, were contributed by Currituck County in order that Dare might become another county, showing pride within itself and taking its proper place among the hundred counties in the historical State of North Carolina. Kitty Hawk remained in Currituck County until 1920, at which time it became a part of Dare County.

During this early period, different parts of Dare County were cut off from each other. The only way to get from Hatteras to Roanoke Island, or to Kitty Hawk or the mainland was by sailboat. George Creef now felt in his weary soul that Dare County had a wonderful future, especially Roanoke Island as well as the beaches. Just as his departed father and mother had predicted, many years ago, before he left his home at East Lake.

Tomorrow was Monday. The day broke gray and misty. George awakened very early and immediately began thinking about his problems. In his mind he began to work out a deliberate course of action because there was no time to lose.

After breakfast, George lost no time sailing out of Shallowbag Bay and across Roanoke Sound to the sound side of the beach where his prize timber was waiting near the edge of the water. George Moore and Mose Midgette had stayed on the island to operate the railway while George Creef was away. Two of the other men, Clyde and Joe, were waiting for George when he arrived to help with the timber.

Chains and dogs were spread out parallel with the shoreline. Soon the mares were hitched to the heart-pine squared logs and at once began pulling them, one by one, out into the shallow water away from the shore until they began to float. The water

94

was almost calm, as the logs took their place side by side in the water.

Then a dog was driven into the outside log, on top, near the end, and all the way across the raft. To those who are not familiar with logging as it was carried on in those days, a dog is a flat iron wedge, sharp at one end, flat and wide at the top, with a strong iron ring fastened through it. The sharp end was driven deep into the log, then a chain was run through these rings, linking them together as they floated side by side, forming a raft. By the end of the following week, five rafts of twenty logs each had been fastened together, anchored near the shore, ready to be moved to the nearest sawmill forty-four miles away.

In August 1871, the Kramers began their lumber business in Elizabeth City, in a three-story building, which stood on the waterfront at the foot of Burgess Street. Later, the Kramer lumber business, known as D. S. Kramer and Sons, was moved to Poindexter Creek property, then known as Kramer Brothers and Company. This took place between the years of 1887 and 1891, when log wagons pulled by a yoke of oxen brought logs by land to their lumber mill.

Kramer Brothers paid their labor fifty cents a day in 1889. Logs in quantities came by rafts pulled by boat, some by barges, and a few by rail, or log wagons. One thing was for sure; in whatever way lumber was brought to the mills, it was very slow and uncertain. Also in 1889, Dr. Oscar McMullan had his office in the rear of the building at the corner of Colonial Avenue and Water Street, where he sold drugs in the front of the building. The place is now known as the City Drugstore.

Later, Kramer Brothers moved the sawmill to what was known as Dry Point, a piece of land next to what is now the residence of Dr. John H. Bonner, on Riverside Avenue, in Elizabeth City, North Carolina. Here the logs were sawed into rough boards, loaded on scows, rowed across the narrow Pasquotank River, under Poindexter Street Bridge, and to the planning mill located on what is now Elizabeth Street. Another planing mill was also located behind what is now the Krueger Chevrolet Company.

Scows were usually about eight feet wide, nearly forty feet long, and generally carried six to eight thousand feet of rough lumber. The scows were moved through the water by means of two large oars sixteen feet in length, with wide blades at one end. The oars were placed in oarlocks, one on each side, and pulled by two strong men.

George waited two long days, for the wind to breeze and blow a steady, brisk pressure against the sails on the two sailboats that were to be used as power to pull the rafts through the water to the Kramer Lumber Company. About midnight the wind shifted, bringing a strong stiff breeze from the northeast. Before daylight, George and Clyde were ready to sail. The rafts began to move away from the pine-fringed trees which dotted the shore-line along the beautiful Roanoke Sound. Moments later, the rafts began to move faster. As they entered deeper water, the wind pressed hard against the sails.

Now and then, through a misty haze, great banks of cumulus clouds threw shadows on the dark water below. On they sailed, out of Roanoke Sound and into the broad Albemarle Sound that lies to the north of Roanoke Island. Suddenly the sun broke through, and the haze disappeared; but not for long, because the day was ending. Gold and crimson splendor of the sunset faded as twilight slowly settled over this part of the earth. Then the grave beauty of the moonlight poured down on the water around them.

At midnight, sails were folded and heavy anchors were thrown overboard to secure the sailboats and rafts. Next morning, George and his companion rose at daybreak and ate cold biscuits and fish from their gallon-tin lard buckets.

It was December 3, 1887, and the sky was clear. Sails were unfurled, anchors were raised as the wind caught against the sails on the small boats, and slowly the rafts began to move ahead. The horizon was red and seeded as the sun rose later in the east, and cast long shadows on these lonely waters.

George stood at the helm, his pipe gripped between his teeth; smoke drifted about in the air from the burning tobacco in the corn-cob bowl. In spite of the facts, he refused to take happenings too seriously because the whole outlook on life is merely a gamble. Today his thoughts were far away.

Murmuring, popping sounds were made by the rolling waves as they sloshed against the boats that moved through the waters of the Albemarle Sound. Clyde had not rested well the night before, and now sat quietly on a low flat box, at the wheel of his sloop, his posture rather drooping. They were only a few minutes away from Point Harbor, which is at the extreme end of Currituck County and at the southernmost tip where the extensive Albemarle Sound washes its shores on the south end, with Currituck Sound on the east that separates the mainland from the beach. But George and Clyde had to sail to the west of Point Harbor, out of Albemarle Sound, on past Powells Point, Jarvisburg, and off Camden Point where North River and the amber water of the Pasquotank River meet. By sailing to the west side of Camden Point, past Old Trap, and Shiloh in the Pasquotank River, would lead them to Elizabeth City, where the Kramer Lumber Company was now operating.

All this reality and detail of the happenings in the past few days engulfed his mind. He hardly noticed the large flocks of wild ducks and geese feeding along the shore in the shallow water as he entered the crossroads where North River and the Pasquotank River come together.

At this point, George and Clyde began discussing these troubled waters, where during violent storms strong winds of hurricane force whipped up heavy seas and whitecaps rode the high rolling waves to the very impressive shoreline along the seemingly endless stretch of lovely washed sand. In the past, at this point where waves rolled high and gust of wind prevailed, many riverboats and a few tugboats have been sunk.

Another day was ending, the weather was favorable, the boats pulled the rafts nearer the shore on the Pasquotank River just off Old Trap, in Camden County, where they were soon safely anchored for the long night ahead.

Perched high at the top of an old swamp cypress tree sat a large bald eagle; a huge, strong bird of prey with sharp vision and powerful wings and claws. Here he sat as if guarding his eaglets. But suddenly he swooped down, then quickly rose up from the ground and back into the air, carrying a baby lamb in his merciless long deadly claws.

The voices of night drew near. The atmosphere was clear, nightfall brought starlight down on the sleeping world as the two men turned to their bunks to rest. The usual sound of the water breaking against the side of their boat, and the whine of the wind through the sails soon lulled them to sleep.

Early the next morning, both men showed satisfaction in their progress so far, with a slight hint of confidence in the expression on their suntanned faces. For breakfast they ate crackers, pork and beans, and drank yaupon. Moments later, sails were made ready and the rafts again began to move through the water.

On and on they sailed, making more progress than was expected. Then time brought another day to a close, now, apparently unconscious of the colorful sunset as it slowly sank toward the dark waters of the Pasquotank River, casting a long, brilliant beam on the soft waves that gently rose and rolled leisurely toward the shore. Such a beautiful picture, with similarity in appearance of a golden stairway to the sky.

Dusk faded as nightfall settled over the area. The evening star twinkled brightly from above, along with millions of other sparkling stars that continuously and freely sprayed starlight on the water. The air was cold; a stiff breeze blew from the northwest. The honking of a gander was loud, sharp, and clear while he stood watch over his flock of wild Canadian geese as they fed not far away.

With their small boats slightly rolling from the low waves, the continuous sound of the water mumbling against the sides of the boat, and the whispering of the wind in the sails lashed to the mast, made the night feel lonely. Three narrow, steep steps led down to the dingy, cold and close space in the bow where they slept. Tonight George took the first watch until midnight.

All too soon the night passed. Both men rose at daybreak, unshaven, cold and tired. Neither ate breakfast but sat watching the first appearance of dawn, as a light streak began to show on the horizon in the east. From the surroundings, no one could have guessed that the season would soon be approaching midwinter.

A round sleepy ball of fire rose slowly above the uneven treetops. Maples, gums, oaks, and cypress trees lined the shore. Leaves purple with gold, reddish brown, some even tinged with green, floated in the russet-colored water alongside the boat. Soon the sails were made ready, and the men were on their way.

Suddenly a loud cracking sound made from the breaking of a large limb, high in a gum tree in the swamp, near the river, caused them to discover the position of a huge black grizzly bear. He was eating juicy blue gum berries from the limb he had broken with his powerful paws and pulled around to him near the body of the leafless tree. The boat moved on; they were nearing the end of their journey. Winter scenery surrounded this extreme part of Eastern North Carolina, where cypress swamps are a place of mystery and strange beauty, and Spanish moss hangs ghost-like from the limbs and branches. The curiously shaped growths, such as cypress knees, which the trees throw up from their roots to get air and sunshine, are used for ornaments.

North Carolina has been noted for its giant cypress trees and juniper swamps since the early days. American pioneers built churches and plantation homes that may be standing many years after our own day. Some of these trees are eight feet in diameter and over a hundred feet tall, with a limb spread of over eighty feet. They are called bald cypress. The cypress doors from some of these trees, used in St. Peter's Church in Rome, served for over eleven hundred years and were still sound when replaced by doors of bronze.

About two hours before sunset, the wind calmed, forcing George and Clyde to drop anchor just a few miles from the Kramer Lumber Company. During the early part of night, the wind began to blow from the east. By noon the following day the breeze grew with intensity. The sails were hoisted, and the rafts moved on down the Pasquotank River. Just before sunset the two small sailboats and their rafts of heart-pine reached the end of their journey and were safely moored near the shore at the Kramer Lumber Company. There they waited until the lumber could be removed from the water, and placed on skids in the lumberyard for a few days so the wind and sun could dry them out before they were sawed into long thick boards.

One thing was for sure. The past seven days had been long and lonely. At last the men breathed a sigh of relief as they munched on large round cookies that the little shopkeeper sold in his store not far from the sawmill. There were no paved streets in Elizabeth City, but plenty of mudholes when it rained, and plenty of dust in dry weather. After making a conscious effort to hear about the trail that George and Clyde had followed, the shopkeeper made a brief statement, confessing without hesitating, that he would keep on selling his cookies at three for a penny.

The sting of winter was felt in the air, as George and Clyde strolled up and down the dusty streets, a few blocks away from the Kramer Lumber Company on Riverside Avenue. On each corner a kerosene lamp in the shape of a lantern, with a transparent case to shield the yellow oil-fed light that reached out for only a short distance into the night, was set on a rather tall pole. Eager to return home and to his own fireside, George paced the cabin floor like one who had very heavy thoughts. Clyde lay snoring in his bunk, tired from the long uncertain journey. Tobacco burning in his pipe blazed brightly as George finally sat down on the edge of his bunk and smoked in silence. The driving passion that he held to build this boat still burned unceasingly.

In the early morning hours, the five o'clock whistle at the lumber yard was frightening as it blew a loud shrilling sound that echoed over the sleepy little town and harbor. Time for the millhands to rise and pack their lunch in small tin pails. Time to begin another day as dawn began to appear over the Pasquotank River. They were also ready to earn another fifty cents in return for their long, hard day's work.

Today greater advantages were soon sensed by George and his tall companion as they sailed away from Elizabeth City, down the reddish dark-brown waters of the beautiful Pasquotank, in a manner that proved that nothing was interfering with their sailboats while the wind held a steady pressure against the sails.

CHAPTER NINE

Their Return

It was a lovely day as George Creef and Clyde, under the pressure of a strong west wind, sailed away from the low flat-top brick, and tin and wood business houses which lined the water-front. Satisfied to escape from the natural beauty of the un-evenly scattered, thin-ferned, browning cypress trees that helped to form the shoreline on each side of the peaceful river as it be-came wider.

Scraggy, moss-covered piling rose a few feet out of the water along the edge of the shore. By eleven o'clock in the morning, the two little proud sloops were leaving the Pasquotank River behind and entering into Albemarle Sound.

The winter sun shone bright overhead in the clear blue sky. Wild geese, ducks, and snow-white swans skimmed the surface of the water as they flew toward the beach. Blue-winged teal made a whistling sound with their wings as they flew swiftly by, barely clearing the masts of the faithful sloops that were plowing through the rushing water of the Albemarle Sound.

Being entertained by the feathered fowls of the sound, and thoughts of returning to their humble homes on this enchanting island enhanced their desire to enjoy the few hours until sunset. The familiar murmur of the water never hushed and seemed to increase against the sides of the boats as they glided through the water, passing Point Harbor, and entered into the open Albemarle Sound which separates Point Harbor from historical Roanoke Island.

Leaving Kitty Hawk, Kill Devil Hill, and Nags Head behind, their home island was now plainly visible to the naked eye. Wild Canadian geese dotted the tall sand hills at Kill Devil Hill and Jockey Ridge, and the sand hills at Nags Head while the sun beamed down on the yellow sand, reflecting a bright golden glare as it sank lower and lower toward the horizon.

Wild ponies, feeding on bushes and water grass along the

sound shore near Nags Head, were undisturbed. Fishing boats, scattered about in the sound, bobbed up and down with the motion of the waves. Clear sight of the island intensified the dark, lonely cedar trees which stood out strikingly in groves on the north end of Roanoke Island—a wavering line that now faded in the distance as twilight settled over this part of the village.

Leaving to the westward was a ray of light, color, and beauty on the darkening horizon from another golden sunset. In a few moments the sailboats entered Shallowbag Bay, on the east side of the island. The wind wrestled with the tall sage grass and water bushes at the edge of the marsh on their left, while they moved through the water in this narrow bay.

Minutes later the boats were once more safely moored at the Water Street dock in Manteo. George looked down the dusty road through the darkness, stretching himself as he stood on the dock before leaving for home.

Seeing the dim yellow light from the oil lamp shining in the narrow window of his home, in the distance, caused him to be more impatient and eager to return to his family. Tired, cold, dirty and unshaven, the men quickly walked home. Clyde lived alone in a shabby run-down shack, not far away from the waterfront.

The sound of George's footsteps on the porch echoed in the living room. Quickly the door was opened. His lovely wife Ann knew him by the sound of his walk. After enjoying a hot home-cooked meal, then they all gathered around the open fireplace, and watched the smoke curl up the stone chimney.

Eagerly the family asked questions about the long, exciting, uncertain and dangerous undertaking. George explained about his trip, and answered all questions as he sipped a hot cup of yaupon and enjoyed the heat from the burning logs.

Around midnight, George stepped outside to get more logs for the fire. While standing beside the woodpile, he examined the sky. No stars were visible and heavy black clouds hovered low overhead, on his face he felt the cold sting of a few snowflakes which had begun to fall. George returned to the fire, breathing heavily from the weight of the logs. He placed them, one by one, on the smoldering remains of the fire.

After the children were all snug in their beds, George and

Ann climbed the gloomy stairway and made their way to the bedroom. Outside the wind roared through the branches of an old tree that grew near the house, while the rustling leaves whispered something through the darkness that filled the room.

On December 7, 1887, George Washington Creef awakened from a deep sleep, into a cold, frozen, snow-covered world. The storm was over; this was the first snow. The intense dead silence was broken by a loud call to breakfast. The smell of freshly perked coffee once again had made its way from the kitchen, into the hall, and up the stairway.

After enjoying another wonderful breakfast, George went outside. His eyes opened wide at the glorious golden shafts of sunlight shining through the forest on the snow-burdened bent treetops and branches. A brown rabbit crouched in the snow-covered grass across the road, nibbling at some grass and warming in the early morning sun. The flutter of quail could be heard while they fed beneath the live oak tree only a short distance away. An icy wind blew through the trees, slightly waving the branches, and huge chunks of frozen snow fell to the ground.

Today George went outside only to get logs for the fireplace, and water from the pitcher pump. Most of the day he spent in planning and drawing the length and width of the new boat that was needed here on Roanoke Island.

George worked and walked among mankind with ears turned to the more realistic problems rather than the roundabout gossip that went on behind his back. From childhood he had been taught the boatbuilding business by his father, at East Lake, and he still had a great love for it.

George strolled toward his railway as the sun blazed down on the frozen little village. The blanket of lovely white crystals, in which Mother Nature had wrapped her world in the quiet hours of the night, had now almost disappeared and left it slushy and muddy underfoot. For four days following the snow, the island had been quiet. No boats had left the docks for the fishing grounds, or the fine oyster beds in Pamlico Sound. But today white sails could be seen across the marshes, beyond Shallowbag Bay, on their way back to work.

George and his men busied themselves with the work that had been left unfinished at the railway, while he was away. As they moved about, large red-winged blackbirds sang their morning

103

song in the rushes nearby. Old Jack stood half asleep on three legs, tied to the corner of the open shed a few feet away from the railway, enjoying the warmth of the winter sun.

At noon, the men stepped from the boat on the railway. Some hurried home to eat; others stayed near Old Jack at the shed, away from the cold north wind, and received the benefit of the sun as they ate fried fish with hunks of cornbread for their dinner.

Across the narrow bay, in the marsh, a cow from a wild herd began to bellow. Clyde was burning to ask questions as he watched the expression on the hard suntanned face of Marcus. Then he saw Marcus reach for his musket and powder bag, and nod.

Clyde understood the gesture. He rose and quickly followed Marcus to a skiff that lay partly out of the water, with its nose resting on shore. Without hesitating, they entered the skiff and swiftly rowed across the bay in the direction of the bellowing beast. From experience, many of these natives knew that one of the herd grazing too near the edge of the water and the boggy marsh had slipped and was mired in the mud. Turning the slight bend around the tall mash grass, they saw a struggling fat young cow. One shot from the musket, and the bellowing was finished.

After a rope was tied over her horns, and then by rowing from one side to the other, snatching and jerking on the rope, the cow was worked loose from the mud. At the railway she was skinned, cut up into beef, and divided among the men. Deer meat was their favorite dish on the island; not many natives hunted wild cattle.

All the men went about their usual duties, no words passing between them; no leisure to brood over anything because Sam, the owner of the fishing boat on the railway, would be expecting it to be repaired and put back overboard by the end of the day, ready to sail out of Shallowbag Bay and into Roanoke Sound to some of the best fishing grounds.

So as the sun sank behind the dark-green treetops, and twilight began to creep over the island, Old Jack held the cable taut around the large winch as he backed little by little until the boat had been moved down the railway and safely into the water.

On February 19, 1888, a letter came addressed to George

Washington Creef Jr. at Roanoke Island, North Carolina, after five days of travel from Elizabeth City to Manteo. In the brief letter, Kramer Brothers Lumber Company informed George that his timber had been sawed into boards, loaded on scows, rowed away to the planers and dressed, and was now ready to be moved back to Roanoke Island.

One side of the large shed at the railway was cleared and made ready to store the valuable lumber out of the weather until it was used.

As Ann read the letter, she smiled with understanding. Now the boat she had heard so much about was becoming more of a reality.

Within the next two days the lumber was towed to Manteo, where it was stored in the shed, beside the railway, ready for use.

For a few feet at one side of the railway, between the shed and the water, the ground lay in uneven ridges divided by washes from heavy rains and high tides during strong south or southeast winds. Low scraggy bushes and trash, such as short ends of rotted boards taken from the boats that were repaired, were soon cleared away. Then the ground was leveled, and a bed arranged in the proper place where the keel for the construction of the new boat was to be laid.

Whatever the risk, George was willing to put every dollar, and all the time that he could spare, without neglecting his railway duties, into this boat.

On May 5, 1888, day broke gray and gloomy. Sea fog moved in from the great Atlantic Ocean.

Across Roanoke Sound it settled over the island powered by a strong, steady east wind.

George, Clyde, and Marcus were at the railway at dawn, more eager than ever to lay the keel. Now it was clear daylight, though the sun had not tipped the tall cedar forest in the east. Only through the heavy fog did any sunlight pass, so that all the rest of the island still lay asleep, while dark-green, mysterious shadowy shapes merged into the walls of the forest as misty and soft as morning clouds.

Hatchets, drawing knives, and adzes were all razor-sharp and ready to begin work on the keel. Long-seasoned white oak lumber of various thickness and width stood on end, ready to be hewed and shaped for the far-reaching sturdy keel. Chips began

105

to fly through the air; mockingbirds were singing as if they wanted everyone to hear them; other birds fluttered and then flew far away.

The fog lifted as the sun rose higher in the sky, and cool breezes blew through the workshed. Scarcely a moment was squandered during the day. After a hard day's work that had a definite purpose, the comfort gave them a personal satisfaction as each went in a different direction toward home.

The wind blew across the waving tops of the live oaks while the light from the setting sun lasted. But soon, with the wind came a shade and a darkening and suddenly the island became gloomy and gray. After the sinking of the golden sun, night came quickly on Roanoke Island among the whispering groves of mystic cedars.

The particulars of this wild environment seemed only the essentials of a strange dream as George stood on his small front porch. He saw the darkening sky, the gray turning black, the tops of the forest moving in waves, like the rippling of waters, and the pointed cedars bowing to each other, while his faithful old deerhounds lay stretched out cozily near him.

Supper was waiting. Ann greeted him with joy and understanding, and listened attentively while George talked about the events of the day, and their daughter Ella played games on the floor. Soon afterward the family went to bed.

George was tired as he lay back, grateful for the comfort of his home and family. The night seemed to steal away from him as he sank softly into the intangible distance of rest and slumber.

George awakened to the sound of his hounds baying a lone black cat sitting high on a fence post. He opened his eyes to another beautiful day. He looked out of the bedroom window at the blue morning sky.

Today Old Jack was allowed to graze freely along the shore and feed on the tender spring grass, under the watchful eyes of the men who were busy shaping the long oak keel soon to be laid a short distance near the railway.

A strong west wind blew down the parched dirt road; now and then a forceful gust dipped down and whirled small clouds of dust about. From time to time George glanced over his shoulder as Old Jack leisurely moved about, bending saplings while he grazed.

Suddenly the horse snorted, raised his head high, and showed signs of excitement. Grabbing his musket, Clyde ran for the shore where Old Jack was backing away. A large brownish water moccasin, measuring five feet in length, with head raised, jaws spread wide showing two long pointed fangs, was ready to strike and inject poison venom into some surprised innocent creature. One shot from the old musket blew the snake to pieces, spattering him into the reddish-brown water in Shallowbag Bay.

The business of repairing boats continued as usual, but every spare moment was spent on the construction of the new boat. On May 20, 1888, the sturdy white-oak keel was laid. It measured fifty-five feet and three inches in length. The men exchanged glances of satisfaction as they left on foot for home.

George Creef welcomed a challenge. From childhood he had been taught to rely on material things—the cold, the heat, the delicious wild fruits, wild animals, and food taken from the waters of the sounds that surrounded this magnificent and mysterious part of the Outer Banks, all of which made life possible in this isolated wilderness.

By noon the next day, at the railway shed, many ribs began to take shape that would some day in the future be fastened and secured firmly to this giant keel. Day after day passed, but not without some progress on his dream boat. Nothing but the finest heart pine and some juniper must be used in building this craft, except the white oak for the keel and ribs to give more strength to the vessel.

CHAPTER TEN

Violent Squall

On August 23, 1888, Amos Hooper, a very close friend from
East Lake, his lovely wife Mary, and their daughter Sue, age
five, came to see George and his family at Roanoke Island. After
supper bits of news were told about the happenings back home
at East Lake, while the children played on the floor. Amos
even mentioned a new industry that had appeared on the scene
at East Lake; it was called "bootlegging," because the people
who made the corn whiskey seldom paid any taxes. In later
years it became known as the "corn likker" capital of the
nation.

During this visit, many things were discussed including Dare
becoming a county in 1870; how Dare was now cut off from the
rest of the state, even from each other here along the Outer
Banks, about 99 percent of the available boats were used only
for commercial fishing, with a few on pilot duty for the inlets.

It was as late as 1850 before the first census was taken, not
only for the population but to show the occupation of the few
residents in the different communities and islands along the
Outer Banks. The census showed that some made their living
from the sea along the beach, while others fished and dredged
for oysters in the channels and in the sounds, and also on the
shallow flats and around the marshes.

Their greatest problem was how to market the fish and oysters
after they were caught. Without transportation and they were
practically isloated from the outside world. This point gave Wash
the long-awaited opportunity to explain the purpose of the boat
that he was now building. The mysterious islands, the blue clear
waters from the Atlantic that wash the sandy Dare beaches, all
offered great opportunities for Dare County.

George and Amos also discussed hunting and fishing, but only
after this problem of transportation was thoroughly aired. With
so much jawing and jousting going on over the island among

108

the natives, George had paid little attention to it because he was too busy at the railway. On and on they talked, exchanging ideas and caching up with the news. Amos was a good listener, and enjoyed being in George Creef's company.

Since the 1830s, Nags Head had been known only to a few Eastern North Carolina people as a summer resort, including Kitty Hawk, and Kill Devil Hills, although only a few of the wealthier families could afford to come. Usually they chartered a flat scow, pulled by a sail or small steamboat, to bring their family, servants, one horse and cart, and a milk cow. Also loaded on the scow were hay, corn, and groceries enough to last through the summer season.

According to the legend that has been handed down for generations, and after personally talking with many of the natives, some of whom were over ninety-three years old, Nags Head received its name from an old horse. In the early days, an old horse or nag, with a lantern tied around his neck, was driven up and down the beach along the surf at night. The swinging motion of the lantern resembled a light from another vessel. Some vessels would steer for it, and beach their ship on the sandbars along the surf. Some history books say the name derived its name from places along the coast of England. Anyway Congress passed a law, in 1825, deeming it a felony "if any person, or persons shall hold out or show any false light, or lights, or extinguish any true light, with the intention to bring any ship or vessel, boat, or raft, being or sailing upon the sea, into danger or distress or shipwreck."

When the conversation began to lag somewhat, George suggested they take a walk in the cool night air. On the two men strolled beyond the grove of live oaks, now and then between the trees, while lights twinkled from candles or oil lamps in the windows. Farther down the dirt road, lights in the windows of the village stores flared more brightly. The sky was changing from gray to blue, and stars began to lighten the blackness overhead earlier than expected. About midnight, all settled down for a good night's sleep.

Dawn broke clear and still, and the day was young when the Creefs walked with their guests toward the dock. Quail fluttered and darted across the path near the road; in the treetops birds sang their early morning song, while in the fresh still air drifted the murmur of the flowing water along the shore of Shallowbag Bay at historical Roanoke Island.

With not enough wind to sail, Amos rowed his small sloop toward the north end of the island, past Mother Vineyard and the beautiful dark-green forest of oaks, scattered pines, and cedars which grew along the tall banks that overlooked Roanoke Sound. Soon the boat left the island behind and entered the Albemarle Sound, running into a mild breeze that began to blow from the north. The sail was unfolded, placed in position, and the boat began to move under its own power. Amos sat at the stern to guide the boat with the tiller which was fastened to the rudderhead.

Around the middle of the afternoon, while Mary and little Sue were enjoying their exciting voyage, black threatening storm clouds began to darken the water. Sharp blinding bolts of lightning streaked across the sky, then suddenly the wind shifted and roared overhead. The small rope that was fastened to the tip end of the boom and usually held in the hand, after being wrapped once or twice around a small cleat on the side of the boat, was made fast to the cleat. The wind blew with great force, and the waves rolled higher. The rope was wet, the pressure of the wind against the sail had tightened the knot.

Amos struggled to untie the knot, but a strong gust of wind struck the sail and overturned the little boat in the rough waters of Albemarle Sound near the entrance to the Alligator River. Thunder rumbled across the sky, trembling the earth around them and causing fear and anxiety while oppressive rains poured down.

Mary had been thrown clear of the boat when it capsized. The rough water was carrying her farther away from the boat, and she screamed for help. Amos sought every ounce of strength in his throbbing body, and swam with unusual haste to her rescue. But only a few feet away from the boat, she sank. The angry muddy waters had claimed her beautiful body.

Amos searched and called for their lovely little Sue, but all in vain. Exhausted and weary, now sure that Sue had joined her mother, he swam back to the sloop that was floating on her side. Now and then high waves washed over him as he desperately clung to an almost submerged useless object.

In about an hour the brief squall was over. The violent wind, driving rain, and rough seas were beginning to cease. Soon blue

110

skies and a brilliant warm sun shone down on this unfortunate tortured soul. It came to him, while he waited, that like the human body the human soul was a strange thing, but could it ever recover from a terrible shock such as he was now experiencing? Only God held the answer.

Another day was ending. Fishing boats returning with their catch were becoming visible on the horizon as they sailed across Albemarle Sound to enter the Alligator River, when the watch on the bow of the *Julie Ann* reported that something was moving in the water dead ahead. The helmsman held his course. Hands were seen feebly waving from the overturned boat. Minutes later Amos was aboard, telling his horrible story.

The crew on the *Julie Ann* helped to right the sloop and bail the water out. Amos stepped down from the *Julie Ann* into his boat and walked forward, when suddenly he screamed, fainted, and fell face down in the bottom.

One of the men rushed to his aid. Kneeling beside Amos, the man saw two bare little feet drawn up against the side of the boat, far up in the covered-over bow.

During the storm, this sweet little angel was probably afraid of the bolts of lightning streaking across the sky, the trembling thunder, the wild roaring wind, and driving heavy rains, and she crouched in the tip of the bow where she felt more secure.

After gently laying her down in the bottom of the sloop, face up, her windblown, water-tangled chestnut curls still beautiful, Amos wept bitterly. Had he known that she was in the bow when his boat overturned he could have easily saved her. But Amos was too busy trying to untie the rope from the cleat so the sail could swing free in the strong wind, and failed to see where she was crouched.

Sorrow quickly spread over the village. Three days later, Mary's body washed up along the shore among the cypress stumps in the Alligator River.

George Creef and his wife Ann were grief-stricken by the tragedy, and spent many hours pondering about the many insecure ways of life.

After the funerals, George and Ann returned to their home on Roanoke Island, ready to gamble with their future against the "hands of time." The next few days were hot, long, and sultry. Late one afternoon, after a hard day's work, George and

111

his faithful workers sat awhile in the shade of the shed to gather strength before going home.

The cool night winds that blew across the water and crept in through the open window as he slept, made him feel greatly refreshed the following morning. He was awakened once again by the mockingbirds singing in the shiny tree, and a blaze of gold rising in the east.

At the railway beside the shed, rib after rib was worked into frame and fastened to the keel; each in its proper place. Narrow strips were made fast to the top of the ribs extending across the keel to the other side, and fastened to the top of the ribs on the opposite side to hold them in place and give them support.

George was chiefly concerned with the present; because the past was history, and the future "no man knoweth." And yet it was the call of the future which stirred him to action. He had no way of knowing what the future had in store for himself or his family, but stubbornly resisted any idea that might appear unexpectedly in his mind and cause him to change his plans or leave Roanoke Island. He had come to stay and to make it a better place in which to live by improving the circumstances.

In the days that followed it became clear that progress was rapidly being made on the new boat as it began to take the form of a skeleton of some large, strange creature. Many long hours were spent in preparing the plank for her sides, and the pitch to waterproof the seams. So far, the weather had been favorable and all went well.

It was no unusual sight late in the evening to watch a deer feeding on the tree-sheltered grass at the edge of the powdery earth road. But today a buck leisurely fed near the back of the yard, while Ann watched from the kitchen window. She waited until the faint slam of a door assured her that George had reached the house and had entered through the front door. Not seeing her, he immediately strolled through the gloomy hallway to the kitchen.

Quickly taking up his rifle, he slipped noiselessly through the bushes down the slight bend in the road, where the deer was slowly moving away under the dark trees at the edge of the grove. The sky was now turning from blue to gray. Stars had begun to lighten the earlier blackness, and from the forest before

112

him blew a soft, cool wind that brought a pleasant scent of wild grapes which hung in bunches from the tree branches.

Keeping close to the edge of the woods, George moved swiftly and silently westward. Suddenly he heard something that brought him to a halt. Cracking noises from small dead twigs underfoot told him that something was coming his way. George sank down low in the gloom, listening and waiting. No more than he had expected judging from the sound, a buck came out of the woods and stopped near the center of the road, motionless, making a perfect target. George slowly lowered his rifle and squeezed the trigger. The deer leaped into the air, then fell to the ground.

George hurried along back to the house. His eyes were keen and used to the dark, but the pale starlight afforded him indistinct sight of the ruts and holes in the road. The shot had been heard by some of the nearby neighbors. When he reached home, help awaited. The women and men had been preparing for the next day, the last Thursday in November, "Thanksgiving Day," dating back to the Pilgrims who came forward spreading their blessings, kneeling and giving thanks to God for their prosperity and happiness.

On this almost hidden island, away from the rest of the world, Ann and George Creef awakened from sleep early in the morning and began thinking about their wonderful blessings on this Thanksgiving Day. From outside, the pleasing sounds pouring from the throats of mockingbirds, and many other various songbirds warbling their morning songs in the branches of the trees near the bedroom window, rang in their ears. They enjoyed the magnificent shafts of bright sunlight shining through the group of trees which stood on the east side of the house. The groves of trees covering Roanoke Island lay shrouded in morning mist, while fleecy white scattered clouds moved slowly and aimlessly in the sky. On the east side the cedar forest was an ornament, a cluster of gold.

At the moment practically all the islanders were busy moving the cooked foods, wild grapes, and fruits and nuts to the long tables which had been built beneath the trees, beside the little church where most of the day was to be spent in prayer and thanksgiving. On the way, robins and brown thrush fluttered among the branches overhead unnoticed by Old Jack, as he walked along at his usual gait. Some of the birds left the branches

113

to flit down and shyly hop near the covey of twittering quail. Brown rabbits crouched in the grass not moving an ear, everything fitted harmoniously into this wonderful scenic, wild, and beautiful island.

At noon the feast started, with first a prayer from the minister. The Lost Colony, which has never been forgotten, was repeatedly mentioned. Only a few months had lapsed since the last gathering on Thanksgiving Day, but so many things had happened, so many memories had come to life and lived in their minds again, only to return to their proper places in the pages of history. It was a great feast, and all enjoyed themselves to the end.

It was late in the afternoon when they departed for home. Dark shadows stretched across the road from the tall trees. An eagle soared overhead, rabbits rustled the dead leaves as they swiftly ran away, and crows flew low above the dark-green cedars on their way to roost. Bushy-tailed squirrels chattered, running from limb to limb in the live-oak acorn trees a short distance away. This had truly been a day of unity, with all the blessings and good tidings, praised in the glorious name of God.

Old Jack had come to a stop. They were home. The dust rising from his hoofs began to drift away in the wind. Later, before the bright blaze from the open fireplace, while shadows danced on the wall about the room, voices gradually became silent. It had been a long day for all.

Next morning, George hurried down the road to the railway and opened the doors to the shed. His fellow workers came down the well-worn trail that led to their work at this extremely difficult task of building a boat of this size so it could be successfully put into operation in the shallow waters of the sounds that surround this famous historical island. Having no accurate method to measure the depth of water that the boat would displace it was very important to select the right thickness, the right weight, and the right kind of lumber that would be durable and long-lasting in spite of hard wear and use.

It was December 20, 1888. The gray gloom of dawn vanished when a red streak began to appear on the rim of the horizon, along the surface of the broad Atlantic Ocean, many thousand miles away. Moments later a large, round, red ball of fire cast brilliant rays on the water. Soon the sky was clear, but the northwest wind was cold. Another typical winter day.

114

George and Ann ate breakfast while the children were still asleep. They discussed family problems, and the possibility that some day the island might become better known to the outside world because they loved the wild and beautiful enchanted surroundings.

In their home, like most other families they had their misunderstandings; but as a rule there was peace and solitude. Their conversation faded as they watched the golden rays of morning sunlight beaming through the kitchen window and across the table where they sat sipping a hot cup of steaming yaupon. Outside, the sighing of the wind through the trees in the forest mingled with sharp chirruping tones of the redbreasted robins.

Another day, resembling many other days, had come and gone. Tools, which had remained idle over the weekend, soon made sounds that echoed against the wall of the railway shed. Through the open door, the forest, glittering with its millions of upturned leaves as the northwest wind tossed them about, bright-faced in the sun, towered upward, crowned with the light blue skies.

A few yards away on Water Street, near the dock, could be seen a slab bearing the words: "Sir Walter Raleigh's Colonists, 1584-1587. Whose friend and guide was the Indian Manteo, christened and called Lord of Roanoke and Pasamonquepeuk, August 13, 1587, in reward of his faithful services." Beside it another stone slab bore the inscription: "To Virginia Dare, firstborn of the English in America, nearby this place. Born the eighteenth and Baptized the twentieth of August 1587, and then vanished with the Colonists." These markers still continue to remain at this historical spot on Roanoke Island, near Shallowbag Bay. The marker, three-and-a-half feet wide and twelve feet high, is built of brick and stone.

Here, only a few years ago, had passed savage tribes of Indians who had roamed this magnificent island, land of enchantment, a dreamer's paradise. Today, friendly people, and beautiful and talented women, are to be found living at this famous site.

Thoughts of those haunting memories were going through George Creef's mind as he worked unceasingly to pave the way that would lead to a better way of living. The rigid mast and boom were carved out of inflexible juniper trees, straight as a line, finished and carefully placed in racks along the wall inside the railway shed.

115

Crows sat on moss-draped limbs in low-fringed cypress trees near the water and stared at the men as they fastened the planks to the ribs and gradually closed in the sides. Kingfishers skimmed the surface of the water, diving now and then for a small fish, and muskrats swam out of their holes beneath the water along the marsh and climbed on tussocks to sun.

Sea gulls followed, hovering near the small fishing boats as they sailed up Shallowbag Bay to the docks at the fish house to sell their catch. Later, George waited for the boats to dock and then bought enough pan mullets for supper. Hardly feeling the weight of another hard day's work, George strolled toward home, glancing upward at the dark overcast now shielding the late afternoon sun. Gold and russet leaves, protected by the thick forest from the icy winter winds, still held their beautiful colors, outlined the sides of the road. For George, the trail ended as he climbed the steps and entered his home.

CHAPTER ELEVEN

Christmas Eve

The next day would be December 24, Christmas Eve. A bright blaze from the roaring fire in the old stone fireplace streaked up the smoke-filled chimney. Outside, large soft snowflakes began to clothe the earth. The wind was still. George occupied an armchair, opposite Ann, who was now on the other side of the room rocking little Hattie. Ella amused herself on the floor near the hearth. By midnight Mother Nature had covered her children with a soft white blanket six inches thick, and disappeared. Stars now sparkled like diamonds in the sky; trees bowed their heads in complete silence and slept.

Next morning broke clear and bitter cold. Later on in the day the children were left at home, while Ann and George went shopping at the village store for candy and toys for Santa Claus. On their way, plowing through the snow on foot, they saw wild turkeys and deer which made scarcely any effort to move where they sheltered from the icy wind, at the edge of the thick growth of trees, enjoying the warmth from the winter sun.

Although many fishing boats needed repairs, for the past two months fishing had been poor and the owners were not financially able to have it done. This left many, including George, in need of money. At the small store George gave Ann all of the money he had to prepare for the event that came only once each year. Ella was now seven, and Hattie was only one year old.

A traveling salesman, better known as a "drummer," came each year to the island and sold many varieties of inexpensive trinkets and toys to the storekeeper. These were to be sold especially during the yuletide season.

The sun sank slowly behind the tall dark-green grove of cedars near the store, bringing an early gloom of twilight over the east side of the island. On entering the store, Ann noticed that extra oil lamps had been placed around the large, dull-looking room to cast more light on the beautiful sparkling trinkets. Over against the wall, colorful dolls with long hair and eyelashes stared with a smile at the customers like little orphans. And when two of these lifelike beautiful little dolls were passed to Ann with arms extended, each one cried "Mama." Ann smiled as she recalled her own childhood days.

Two dolls, two cone-shape horns, two boxes of sparklers, a few Christmas apples, and a pound of fine candy were all placed in a paper box, and tied with a string from a ball of twine that hung in a round basket-shaped holder which extended from the ceiling.

On their way home, back down the snow-covered trail, lights from nearby houses glowed through the partially snow-covered windows. Saw-toothed icicles clung to the narrow window sills. Crust on the surface of the snow-covered frozen ground made a crunchy sound underfoot with every step.

Ella, hearing her mother make thumping noises while removing the snow from her high-top shoes, flung open the door and immediately asked for candy. Her father, entering the back door, crept quietly through the kitchen, hid the box in the room next to the hall, behind the door, and covered it with some old clothing. Then he quietly slipped through the hallway, and entered the living room unnoticed while Ella sat near the fireplace crunching on her candy.

Some minutes later, Ann opened the family Bible in her lap and began reading to the children, explaining about the birth of Jesus. Ella, only seven, sat very still and eager to hear. Softly Ann began to tell them the story of Christmas.

Now the Lord said unto Abraham, who was one of God's chosen people: Get thee out of thy country, and from thy kindred, and from thy father's house, go into a land that I will show you. And I will make of you a great nation. I will bless you, and make your name great, and thou shalt be a blessing unto your people. I will bless them that bless you, curse them that curseth thee, and in thee shall all families of the earth be blessed.

So Abraham departed as the Lord had spoken unto him. Abraham was seventy-five years old when he obeyed God and departed out of Haran. He took his wife Sarah, Lot and his brother's son, and all their belongings that they had gathered together, all the souls Abraham had gotten in Haran, and they all went forth to go into the land of Canaan.

(For the benefit of my readers, especially those who have not had the opportunity around the world to have been taught about the birth of Jesus, there were forty-two generations from the time of Abraham until Christ was born. The birth of Jesus was from the works of God.)

When Mary was to marry Joseph, before they came together she found that she was to have a child of the Holy Ghost. Then Joseph, her husband, being a just and righteous man, not willing to make her a public example, was thinking about putting her away privately. But while he thought on these things, behold, the angel of the Lord appeared unto him in a dream, saying: Joseph, thou son of David, fear not to take unto thee Mary thy wife; for that which is conceived in her womb, is of the Holy Ghost. And she shall bring forth a son, and thou shalt call his name Jesus, for he shall save his people from their sins.

Now all this was done, that it might be fulfilled which was spoken of the Lord by the prophet, saying: Behold, a virgin shall be with child and bring forth a son, and they shall call his name Emmanuel, which, interpreted, means God is with us. Then Joseph awoke from his sleep and did as the angel of the Lord had commanded him to do, and took unto him his wife. He knew her not in the manner of man and wife until she had brought forth her firstborn son.

Ella now sat close to her mother on a little low round-top stool that her father had made for her in his shop some time ago. Little Hattie was fast asleep. Ann asked Ella to listen carefully and she would soon hear why there was a Christmas and a Santa Claus. She began again:

It came to pass in those days that there went out a decree from Caesar Augustus, that all the world should be taxed. (This tax was first made when Cyrenius was governor of Syria.) So all went to be taxed, every one into his own city. Joseph and Mary also went up from Galilee, out of the City of Nazareth, into Judea, unto the City of David, which is called Bethlehem—because Joseph was of the House, and a direct descendant of David—to be taxed with Mary his wife, who was great with her child (soon to be born). And so it was that while they were there, the day came for her child to be born. She brought forth her first born son, and wrapped him in swaddling clothes (long narrow bands of cloth) and laid him in a manger because there was no room for them in the Inn (or small hotel).

There were shepherds in the same country, waiting in the fields and keeping watch over their flocks by night. Some shepherds watched over their sheep, some over their cattle, and some kept watch over their camels. And lo, an angel of the Lord came to them, and the glory of the Lord shone all around them, and they were filled with grief and were afraid. Then the angel said unto them: Fear not, be not afraid, for behold, I bring you good tidings of great joy which shall be to all people. For unto you and all people is born this day in the City of David a savior, which is Christ the Lord, and this shall be a sign unto you: You shall find the infant babe wrapped in swaddling clothes, lying on hay in a manger, in the stable behind the Inn.

Suddenly there was with the angel a large number of the heavenly host praising God and saying: Glory to God in the highest, and on earth peace and good will toward men. It came to pass, as the angels were gone away from them into heaven, that the shepherds said to each other: Let us go now even unto Bethlehem and see this thing that has come to pass, which the Lord has made known unto us through his angels.

They came into the city with haste and found Mary and Joseph, and the baby lying in a manger. When they had seen it, they made known far and wide the saying which was told to them by the angels concerning this child. All the people that heard it wondered at those things which the shepherds told them.

But Mary kept all these things and pondered them in her heart. The shepherds returned to their flocks, glorifying and praising God for all the things that they had heard and seen as it had been told unto them. The baby Jesus grew and increased in strength, and became strong in spirit.

"Now you see," said Ann, "why we have a Christmas. It is Jesus' birthday. Without this glorious gift from God, our Father, there would be no Christmas."

The clock on the shelf over the fireplace struck eleven times. Two long white stockings were hung at each end of the mantle-piece, near the corner of the worn edges, with the feet hanging, about twelve inches above the warm stone hearth.

While Ann was coming to the end of the story about Santa

Claus, and his reindeers with large-branching antlers, pulling a sleigh full of toys over the frozen snow, sleigh bells ringing, and Old Santa dressed in his red suit trimmed with white fur, this little angel fell fast asleep with her head resting on her mother's knee.

George picked up Ella in his arms, climbed the old stairway to the top. Ann followed close behind carrying little Hattie.

A large orange ball that earlier had risen in the east, had now changed its color to bright yellow as it sailed in the sky above the beauty of this strange island, casting moonbeams through the upstairs window and furnishing enough light by which to tuck in two little angels for the night. Then Ann and George tiptoed across the narrow hallway to their own bedroom.

While still sitting on the side of the bed, George congratulated Ann on the teaching from the Holy Bible to Ella. He also had enjoyed every word of it as he sat staring into the open fireplace and puffing at his corn-cob pipe.

Outside the sky was clear, the moon was full, and brilliant moonlight fell on the dark shadows of the scattered houses, and the trees in the forest quietly slept beneath the blanket of snow.

George fell asleep still wrestling with the old familiar urge to see his boat finished, still soberly pondering over her future.

Early the next morning, George stepped out into the open air. The lazy morning sun was warm. By noon, large chunks of frozen snow were falling from the trees to the ground.

Ann worked leisurely about the house. The children played happily with their toys. The afternoon and evening they spent together by the fireside, while the burning hickory logs furnished heat and light, and added beauty to the living room.

Christmas had come and gone. Winter was nearly over. Ice and snow seemed to have departed George and his fellow workers stood in the doorway of the workshed at the railway, watching another glorious crimson and gold sunset. Streams and brooks that once stood still now made continuous murmuring sounds, while the running water babbled over obstacles as it rushed toward the bay. Numerous birds and wild animals were becoming more active, mating and moving in and out of the forest.

Day by day the men worked hard and continuously, with faithful Old Jack standing by always ready to do his duty when called upon. It was March 31, 1889, and spring had come once again. March flowers, or jonquils, outlined the border of the small front yards with a roll of yellow gold. Down at the railway could be seen a sea of purple violets as they raised their heads, slightly nodding in the light breeze that blew from the south.

For the next two months, commercial fishing was excellent. Many large catches were brought in to the fish houses to be sold. Boats that had been in need of repairs were now keeping Old Jack busy pulling them out of the water and up on the railway. By the middle of June, most of the fishing and oyster boats had been repaired, or painted, and the railway was quiet once more. This gave George and his men practically full time to work on the new boat, which was nearing completion.

During July and August the days were hot but long, giving them still more daylight to work on the boat. Every plank fitted to the frames along the sides, around the stern, and on the deck, was carefully examined before caulking the seams and being treated with pitch to preserve the wood and prevent leakage.

Many of the natives stood a short distance away, staring and mum, though some asked questions, while the mast was raised and put into place. No doubt uncertainty filled the minds of these people, judging by the questions that were asked, whether this wonderful boat, when loaded, would successfully operate in some of these shallow waters in the sounds that surrounded this magnificent Island.

Soon the headstay was fastened to the mast, then to the bow, and made secure. Using the halyard, George Creef raised the mainsail as the boom swung in an unhurried manner but unable to relax. Then the rudder—or flat, movable piece of board hinged vertically to the stern of the boat and used for steering and controlling it while underway—was hung in the large eye bolts, and immediately began to swing from one side of the stern to the other in flawless harmony.

All planks, each one-and-a-half inches thick and three inches in width, that were fastened to the sides, around the stern, and on the deck with copper nails and wooden pegs, were cautiously inspected. Every workable part was now in its proper place. Friends and foes alike stood watching and mumbling, and many remarks were whispered; some were harsh, others humorous. Some edged closer and reached out eager hands to touch the

122

sides of this splendid sailboat. Cattle wading along the shore, feeding on drift grass near the water's edge, raised their heads to stare at the gathering before vanishing into the thick undergrowth.

But on went the progress, moving forward to completion and perfection.

During this same summer of 1889, after more than half a century had lapsed into silence, an aged, wrinkled, sick old woman with barely enough strength to walk, still lived alone in her small exposed and roughly built cottage at Nags Head, North Carolina.

While the summer colony activities were at their peak, this very old lady was found scarcely alive, lying on her bed. One of the teen-age boys, while prowling about the beach, looked inside the seemingly deserted shack, and found her mumbling and begging for help.

Quickly he ran over the wind-blown sand dunes and through the scattered beach grass to the summer cottage of Dr. William G. Pool, one of the summer residents at Nags Head, who lived with his family in the cottage he had built in 1855. Soon Dr. Pool was at her bedside, and immediately began to treat her for some kind of fever. Seeing that she was alone, he spent most of the day waiting for her to respond to his medical treatment.

While waiting, Dr. Pool noticed a beautiful hand-painted portrait, in color, of a spirited and vigorous young woman, supporting every indication of refinement. He also gazed at many dusty expensive silk and satin dresses, including gorgeous evening gowns. Some were hanging on the gloomy, dingy wall, others were scattered about the room.

The old lady began to mumble, then she spoke more clearly. She told Dr. Pool that she was ninety-three years old, and how much she appreciated his help. Cautiously he asked who she was. She refused to say, but forced a smile upon her strange wrinkled face. The next few moments passed in silence. Then Dr. Pool inquired about the costly beautiful dresses and the expensive earrings she was wearing in her pierced ears.

When she could sit on the edge of the bed she seemed to look deep into the past, and finally the old lady began to unravel the tangled memories in her past. The best that she could re-

123

member was that the United States and England were having trouble and finally ended in a war.

About that time, after a northeast storm of the night before, a small sailing schooner came ashore at Nags Head with no one aboard. After hesitating a few moments, she then told Dr. Pool that she had waded ashore. Suddenly the conversation stopped, but Dr. Pool then asked her to tell him all that she could remember.

From the expression on her face, she seemed to be more at ease, and the old lady resumed her story. She had waded out a short distance from the sandy beach and called, but there was no answer. Only the unceasing sound of the breakers as they rolled toward the shore, and the piercing sound of the sea gulls that aimlessly flew back and forth low overhead.

According to her story, she had climbed aboard the schooner and found all of these valuable belongings. After bringing them ashore, she had kept them in her possession ever since that terrible tragedy. Dr. Pool listened with great interest while she pieced the series of events together.

Shyly telling Dr. Pool that she had no money, she asked whether for his pay he would accept the portrait hanging on the wall. This was all she had to offer for his medical assistance. But he refused, telling her that he was pleased to be available. Slowly she rose from her bed, made her way across the stuffy and untidy little room, and removed the picture from the wall. Her hands trembled as she pressed it into Dr. Pool's hands, and insisted that he take it with him as a gift.

Outside, Dr. Pool's horse and beach cart were waiting. Before leaving, he promised that he would take good care of the picture. This seemed to please the old lady very much. Then, closing his satchel, he bid the old lady farewell and left.

A few days later, Dr. Pool inquired among the natives at Nags Head about the schooner which the old lady had mentioned. But no one had ever heard of a schooner of that description coming ashore at Nags Head or at any other place on the beach along the Outer Banks. The story that the old lady had told began to puzzle the doctor very much. But the more he examined the picture, the more he was convinced that it was the work of a great artist and that the painting was that of a very prominent young woman of the wealthy fashionable class.

Dr. Pool became interested in the beautiful picture, and when the summer residents were ready to return home—with their milk cow, horse, and chickens—he took the picture with him, back to his plantation home—known as "The Eyrie Plantation"—near Elizabeth City, North Carolina.

The next three years passed rather quickly for Dr. Pool. He was kept busy tending to his patients, and beginning to feel his age. One afternoon, while he was discarding some old magazines, he came across an old story written about Aaron Burr.

Turning the thin, crumbling, faded, brown pages he found Aaron Burr's picture. Beside him stood a very beautiful young woman. The picture had lost its color and freshness, but something began to stir in his memory, bringing back past events.

Suddenly his curiosity was greatly aroused as he noticed the hair style, the innocent lovely brown eyes, and fair complexion. Also the firm round protruding bosom. Dr. Pool went hastily to his study where this marvelous portrait of some lovely woman hung on the wall. As he entered his study through the open door he glanced at the picture he had accepted as full payment for urgent medical services at Nags Head, North Carolina, a few years earlier.

On comparing the two pictures, he was sure that they were of the same lovely young woman, Theodosia Burr, although they had been made a few years apart. Without delay, Dr. Pool sent many articles to various magazines and newspapers, seeking persons related to Aaron Burr. Many replies came to his home at the Eyrie Plantation, and two actually came in person. Charles Burr Todd, and Stella Darke Knaplin, descendants of the Burr and Edwards families. With them they brought a picture of Theodosia, that had been treasured in their possession for many years.

After comparing every possible feature, along with that of Dr. Pool's painting, they all quickly agreed and were thoroughly convinced that the painting was Theodosia Burr Alston.

Now the mystery was—how truthfully did it get into the possession of this aged, unknown sick woman at Nags Head, North Carolina. Who was this old lady? Many conflicting stories have been told about her—though actually there was no proof—such as an old man of eighty-seven confessing on his deathbed that he had been on the pirate ship which captured the small sailing schooner, and had held a thick narrow plank while the brave young woman was forced to walk overboard; that she had asked no mercy and was calm, but requested that her father and her husband be notified of her destiny.

And there were other confessions made by different persons as to her whereabouts; but until this day no one has ever been able to prove what really happened. It still remains one of the many unsolved sea mysteries among the ill-tempered vast Atlantic Ocean, and the dangerous coastline along the Outer Banks of North Carolina.

Today the mysterious portrait of a spirited young woman hangs in the MacBeth Art Gallery, in New York City, and those lively vivid brown eyes stare at all who pass by.

CHAPTER TWELVE

The Launching

On September 12, 1889, George Washington Creef Jr. and his fellow workers were happier than they had ever hoped to be in their lives as they stood near the railway gazing at the completed and beautiful one-mast sailboat, which measured fifty-five feet, two inches in length, and eighteen feet, four inches in breadth. The bottom was almost flat, slightly V-shaped at the center along the beam; some called her the "Bug-Eye" type.

One deck, one mast, a sharp bow, one large open hatch, and a round stern. On each side of her bow, and on her stern, the name "*Hattie Creef*" was proudly displayed. She was named in honor of George's daughter, Hattie. After almost sixteen months of hard work, the *Hattie Creef* stood ready to be launched.

Four long, slender pine trees were cut and skinned. By removing the bark, the slippery sap slowly oozed from the log. These skids were placed a few feet apart; one end under the boat, and the other end, slightly sloping, rested on the railway, making it easier to slide the sailboat on the skids and over on the railway cradle so she could be launched.

The warm September sun sank slowly behind the dark-green trees in the west; a cool wind, blowing from the northeast, made the nights more pleasant. Many natives watched and were eager to see the *Hattie Creef* launched. Curiosity mounted as to whether there would be enough water for her to be usable in Shallowbag Bay or in many other places of shallow water in the sounds that surrounded this historical island where the Lost Colony had so mysteriously disappeared in the recent past.

George strolled homeward along the dusty road the Indians had trod for so many, many years. After supper he climbed to the top of the rickety old stairs and went to bed. He was awakened about daybreak by the blue jays squalling, woodpeckers hammering on dead trees, and squirrels chattering on the ground, while the wind whined in the pine tops across the road and whispered softly under the eaves of the roof near the bedroom window.

In the kitchen below, a pot of yaupon steamed on the stove, biscuits browning in the oven and ocean spots frying in the pan over the roaring fire mingled and gave out a pleasing aroma that filled the room. Light from the kerosene lamp on the table against the wall gave more light to the room than usual, while Ann and her husband ate an early breakfast.

Afterward George went to the door. Outside, he could not see far in the gloom because of the storm that hovered over the island. Today the wind blew from the north, and he felt a fine cool mist on his tanned face as he closed the kitchen door. Soon large drops of rain beat on the roof, the wind mourned around the corner of the house. George drew short puffs on his pipe causing round masses of smoke to drift about the room. No launching today.

September 14, 1889, the day broke clear with blue skies overhead. A crimson streak blazed on the horizon in the east. Moments later, a round ball of fire began its journey across the sky.

Convinced that the *Hattie Creef* would be all that he expected, everything was made ready for the launching, while Old Jack stood by. George began sliding the sailboat on the skids toward the railway with Old Jack's help, also the help of many of the islanders who came to watch and help with the launching. By noon the boat was resting on the cradle, ready to be let down into the water.

While Old Jack kept the steel cable taut around the large iron winch, backing slowly as she started moving toward the reddish-brown water in Shallowbag Bay. In a matter of minutes, the cradle disappeared beneath the water, while the *Hattie Creef* swung slightly with the tide and from the pressure of the steady stiff breeze that blew from the north.

The small crowd of natives stood along the shore and cheered, as she floated somewhat like a cork, shaped like a huge duck, with a draft (or depth of water that she displaced) being only three feet and three inches. Overhead, the bright sun smiled down on the island and the *Hattie Creef* as the celebration began. By midafternoon several trial runs had been completed in the Roanoke Sound, with all doubts as to her expectancy and service in these waters completely erased from their minds. Ann was

128

pleased with the expression on her husband's tired face.

When the *Hattie Creef* was secured at her mooring for the night, George and his family briefly glanced back at the boat that seemed so much alive, then left for home as dark shadows slowly crept over the rough dusty road, and the sun sank behind the uneven deep-green groves of trees. Birds were swallowed up by the dense darkening forest as they flew inside its mouth. Squirrels chattered from the live oaks, acorns bounced in the autumn leaves on the ground, and a rabbit suddenly jumped and ran into the woods. Quail bunched for the night and began to twitter in the tall broomstraw near the road.

Home again, George and Ann discussed the possibilities of using the *Hattie Creef* on the rich oyster beds in Pamlico Sound, while the children listened and played with their toys. Then they all retired for the night.

The fine large oyster beds that produced these luscious-tasting oysters, like the fishes of the sea, the sounds and the rivers have been there for many centuries. During the next four weeks the sailboat was fully equipped for the undertaking or task.

On October 18, 1889, the morning was beautiful. Fall flowers with their bright blossoms stood up among the dying clumps of grass and swayed in the north wind. Voices of birds were amusing and sweet on the morning air.

While walking toward the dock at the foot of Water Street, George confessed to himself that he loved this thickly forested island inhabited mostly by wild game and full of hiding places. He gazed at the sea of treetops, so bright and green were the cedars, pines, and live oaks, while the maples and others reflected an image of a typical autumn day, displaying their purple, red, orange, and gold leaves in the path of the rising sun.

Soon the sail was hoisted, and the *Hattie Creef* was slightly turned to starboard to catch the pressure of the steady wind that blew out of the north against the sails. Suddenly she began to move, then quickly picked up speed as she sailed out of Shallowbag Bay, through the narrow creeks by the marshes, and soon left the south end of Roanoke Island behind, heading for the oyster beds in the broad Pamlico Sound.

Grappling with the iron tongs for several hours, she was soon loaded with oysters. George and Clyde were very happy with their catch when they tied up alongside the dock at Manteo as twilight settled over the island. Meantime Ann was kept busy with her work at home and the rearing of their two little girls.

On December 3, 1892, Ann gave birth to her third child. They named the boy Hubert Augustus Creef.

For the next few years, the *Hattie Creef* was used on the oyster beds, also for commercial fishing, and especially during the shad season. She proved to be very efficient, except for one detail on the oyster beds. She was considered light, strong, easy to control, and did an excellent job dredging for oysters while going with the wind or having a fair wind. But then she had to tack in order to get back into position to dredge again. This took too long, especially when the wind lacked the strength to force effective pressure against the sails. This was not the proper place for the *Hattie Creef*.

On April 1, 1899, George Washington Creef, Jr., sailed the sloop into Shallowbag Bay, and made her fast to her mooring near the railway. Old Jack rolled his eyes in greeting as he champed on tender green grass. George walked up the muddy road as the sun sank behind the treetops casting long dark shadows on the ground. Ann opened the door as George climbed the steps to the porch. She noticed the worried expression on his suntanned face, but no questions were asked.

Later, George told her in detail about his recent experiences with the *Hattie Creef* under certain weather conditions. With little encouragement from his faithful wife, he decided to put the boat back on the railway, make some changes, and use her for the purpose for which she had been intended from the beginning.

Early the next morning, before dawn, Old Jack was once more called on, and the *Hattie Creef* was soon out of the water and back on the cradle, dripping and drying out, while the early morning sun rose slowly above the marsh, as the sage, rushes, and cattail flags rustled in the breeze.

Plans had been carefully checked for the changes that were to made. Work immediately began on deck, from the center of the boat toward the aft end, to construct an oval-shape room for passengers' convenience and enjoyment, by lowering the deck floor in the stateroom down into the hole of the boat, low enough to allow the boom to barely clear the top as it swung from side to side while changing courses underway. Wall benches, or long seats made of wood, soon occupied every bit of space around the wall, securely fastened to the sides and supported by legs, a few feet apart, resting on the floor. This left the center of the state-room clear for anyone who might wish to entertain the passengers when underway.

Singing and yodeling were very popular with the natives on the island along with guitar, mouthharp, and other musical in-struments. Beneath the pilot house, a small galley, or ship's kitchen, was used to prepare meals for the passengers and crew. One berth inside the pilothouse was neatly fastened to the wall, and two berths, and one toilet were soon ready for use in a small interior space, enclosed by walls, back of the pilothouse, with one door opening out on deck.

Below deck, a large hollow space was left to be used for carrying freight. The mail was kept inside the pilothouse of this well built sailboat. Every drift bolt, every section that was hewn out of juniper logs from the famous juniper swamps in North Carolina, and every virgin heart-pine board used from the begin-ning in the construction, had been thoroughly checked and found to be in excellent condition.

On December 20, 1899, George and his men finished painting the *Hattie Creef* snow-white; the trim work was painted jet black. A few hours later, in the afternoon, she was launched and made ready for her first voyage as a passenger, mail, and freight boat. She was to sail early the next morning from Manteo, at the foot of Water Street on Roanoke Island, to Elizabeth City, which was about forty-four miles away.

Many islanders stood on shore and admired her. She resembled a huge white swan, as she swung leisurely with the tide, secured to her mooring at the dock. A large round red and orange ball of fire, hung low in the distance over the road, had just begun to sink behind the pointed tufts of cedar groves in the forest, and the harsh cry of a crow was heard among the trees as George set his feet into motion on his journey home.

That night Captain Martin Johnson was told that the next morning he would sail the *Hattie Creef* and her cargo to Eliza-beth City. He would have the help of Lee Dough, the cook and deckhand. After going to bed, he lay a long time awake in won-dering joy and happiness as the hands of time worked their way toward a realization of his responsibility.

131

The next morning Captain Johnson awoke before dawn, just before the time when light first appears. With so little sleep, when he awoke it seemed some sort of a dream. But the sound of wind in the trees outside, and the fierce bark of a neighbor's dog told him that dreams must give way to the coldest, rational, reality of sensible thinking. Captain Johnson knew his job, and he also knew that he was big enough for it.

When Captain Martin Johnson arrived at the dock, twenty passengers were waiting, a small canvas bag filled with mail was passed to him to be locked in the wall cabinet of the pilothouse, boxes of fish were soon loaded, and he had orders for merchandise to be brought back for the general store at Roanoke Island.

At 5:00 A.M., December 21, 1899, the sails were unfurled and orders given to shove off. Shallowbag Bay was narrow; marshland ran parallel with the uneven shoreline on the east side of the island for some distance toward the north end, but ended before coming abreast of Mother Vineyard and boldly joined Roanoke Sound.

The wind blew from the east against the sails as the *Hattie Creef* moved slowly away from her resting place. Wild hollyhocks, tall with white and red flowers, gave a striking appearance as they slept near the water along the edge of the marsh. Stars still shone in rapid intermittent gleams overhead; the sting of winter was felt in the early morning air.

Soon a light streak gradually appeared on the horizon, pushing back the darkness that covered the island. Half a mile down the bay and out in Roanoke Sound, along the high banks, rose the lofty groves of trees. Ferns and moss overhung the banks, wild ducks dotted the sound, and kingfishers darted about the surface of the water.

The rushing of the water against the sides of the boat as she smoothly glided through the open space, along with the honking noise of the wild geese that flew low, barely skimming the face of the water close by, all broke the silence and filled their ears. A strange feeling crept over Captain Johnson as he glanced back at this magnificent island, left as nature had made it, with its mysteries, it made him shiver.

The glorious sunlight and warmth of the winter sun were welcome as a steady strong wind blew icy spray across the deck from the whitecaps mounting the open waters of Albermarle

Sound. All seemed to be enjoying themselves, and thrilled at the thought of having transportation from Roanoke Island to Elizabeth City at such a low cost. Fare for the passengers was one dollar and twenty-five cents, and fifty cents extra for their meals, which included all they could eat with brown biscuits and hot yaupon.

Young lovers sat on deck, cuddling against the leeward side of the stateroom, sheltered from the wind, while Captain Johnson proudly sailed the *Hattie Creef* across the spacious Albermarle Sound. He whistled softly as he stretched his cramped body while sailing to the left of Point Harbor at the extreme south end of Currituck County. Soon they passed Powells Point, then Jarvisburg and Grandy piers, all on his right, which ran out into deeper water away from the shore on the west side of Currituck County.

On the *Hattie Creef* sailed, soon entering the waters where the Pasquotank and North rivers meet, running together off Camden Point, which is the south end of Camden County. From time to time the passengers came on deck for a brief stay, listened to the strong east wind whining in the sails, felt the cold sting in the air, watched the beautiful irregular shoreline along the Pasquotank River, sprawling with ferned and moss-draped cypress trees washed by the amber-colored water of the river.

Strange beauty was seen as they passed Hospital Point. Curious growths like cypress knees, which the trees throw up from its roots, and ghostlike Spanish moss that hung from the branches as the *Hattie Creef* entered where the river began to narrow and led to the docks near which low flat top-wood and brick buildings stood along the waterfront. Barges loaded with logs and towed by small tugs moved slowly through the water as Captain Martin Johnson sailed his boat into the harbor.

At 10:30 A.M. the *Hattie Creef* was made fast to the piling at the Nathan Grandy Dock, near the narrow crudely built wooden bridge—a link between Camden County and Elizabeth City, across the Pasquotank river where the river was very narrow but deep. Many people were on hand to greet Captain Johnson and his people, and see this wonderful boat from the distant and isolated part of North Carolina. The sailboat filled a great gap between the Outer Banks and Elizabeth City, where

133

the Norfolk & Southern Railroad Company operated passenger and freight cars that ran in different directions for the public's convenience.

The passengers quickly went about their task in a busy manner, loading bags of coal, groceries, clothing, mail, and many other items, while the Stars and Stripes, displayed at the top of the mast, proudly waved and fluttered in the breeze. By 1:30 P.M. everyone was ready to return to his native island. No one had taken time out to eat. Orders were given to shove off, and while dinner was being served, the *Hattie Creef* moved down the river under full sail.

A short time after leaving the dock, some tacking was necessary in order to get the force of the wind against her sails. Frequently Captain Johnson was forced to change the course of his vessel until they passed Hospital Point, where the Pasquotank River widened over a relatively large area, to a position where he could make a turn slightly to starboard and set a southeast course. The wind blowing from the east would give plenty of wind in her sails, forcing her to move swiftly down the dark choppy waters of the river, on passed Camden Point, and entering the easily disturbed Albemarle Sound.

Two large round vents, one on each side of the vessel, provided plenty of ventilation below. Delicious fried chicken, cooked the Southern way, potato salad, light-brown gravy with hot biscuits, and plenty of steaming yaupon was enjoyed by all.

(Just a little tip for some of you younger ladies, about the Southern Fried Chicken that you hear so much about—the kind that you don't need dog-teeth to chew with, the kind that you hear so much about all over the country. If you want to convince your skeptical husbands beyond any reasonable doubt that the chicken he bought with his hard-earned money is in good hands, and that you are the best cook in the whole world, listen to this:

Cut up your chicken into separate pieces, place them into any ordinary pot, add enough water to cover, and include a dash of salt. Then place the lid on the pot, and parboil until it is tender. This you will know when you stick a two-pronged cooking fork into the chicken, and the meat falls off without having to be pulled off. Lose its flavor? No! Now mix a batter: an egg or two, plain flour, half water and half evaporated milk in the mix, a dash of salt, and beat until thoroughly mixed. It should be just thick enough to stick when the chicken is dipped in it. Remove the chicken from the pot, out of the water, before starting to fry it. This gives it chance to dry out so the batter will stick to it more easily. Place the batter-dipped pieces in a pan of hot cooking oil, and fry until golden brown. *Now* you have Golden Brown, Southern Fried Chicken that will melt in your mouth. And I'll just bet you young brides that this gets you an extra sweet little kiss. Remember, most husbands are expecting that chicken to bounce back every time they try to chew it.)

The weather was clear but cold. The *Hattie Creef* sailed out of the Pasquotank River and into the spacious Albermarle Sound, once more passing the shores on the west side of Currituck County where the long piers ventured out from the shores, exposed and scarred by the sheets of ice that form on the surface of the water during bitter cold winter months. At this time transportation was poor, small freight boats stopped at Newberns Landing, at Powells Point, Jarvisburg, and Grandy piers to load potatoes and other farm produce to be carried to the docks at Elizabeth City, where it was transfered to boxcars which stood waiting on the railroad tracks near the docks ready to take all shipments by rail to large Northern cities.

All these lovely sights gradually disappeared on the horizon as Roanoke Island slowly became more clearly visible about five degrees off the port bow. Large high, barren, sand hills reflected the light from the slanting sun. All too soon this wonderful day of sightseeing, shopping, singing and laughter was ending. The sun was spraying a golden stream of light on the water, brightening the steep colorful banks along the shore on the north end of Roanoke Island, where haunting memories penetrated deep into the forest.

Captain Johnson suddenly swung the bow of the *Hattie Creef* toward the southeast and tacked around the east side of the island for a few minutes, then back parallel with the shore where she soon entered Shallowbag Bay. Twilight had gathered under the high banks, loneliness shrouded the wild groves of slender trees that grew near the shore on this mystic island. Pine tops swayed tirelessly while the wind created a harmonious musical melody whispering through the leaves. Stars began to show; at first pale, then bright. Orders were given to lower the sails.

135

Many natives stood waiting along the dock at Manteo, eager for her return. It was 5:30 P.M. The *Hattie Creef* was a great success. Transportation and communication had dipped to their lowest ebb during the turn of the century for the natives who lived, isolated, along the coast of North Carolina on the Outer Banks.

For the next ten months Captain Martin Johnson and Lee Dough sailed the *Hattie Creef* from Manns Harbor and Manteo to Elizabeth City, carrying freight, passengers, and mail, and making the run twice each week.

CHAPTER THIRTEEN

Creative

In 1850, when Milton Wright was twenty-two years old he was ordained as a pastor in the United Brethren Churches. Nine years later, at the age of thirty-one, he married Susan Katherine Koerner, age twenty-eight. At this time they lived in Indiana.

On April 16, 1867, Wilbur was born. Then, in 1869, the Reverend Milton Wright moved his family to Dayton, Ohio, where he became the editor of a church publication, *The Religious Telescope*. Susan had two other sons, Reuchlin and Lorin, twins born after Wilbur. The twins died.

In Dayton, Ohio, their fourth son, Orville, was born in August, 1871. Also in Dayton, exactly three years after Orville's birth, Susan gave birth to her only daughter. They named her Katharine. While Wilbur and Orville were very young, the Wright family had begun to be creative.

Their mother, Susan, made the children funny-shaped toys and playthings while their father was busy with his duties. In 1877, the Reverend Wright was promoted to the rank of Bishop. The next year he was sent to Cedar Rapids, Iowa. His family remained in Dayton until 1881, then they moved to Richmond, Indiana.

Three years later the family moved back to Dayton. So you can see that with such frequent changes of residence the Wright family became unusually close. Both Wilbur and Orville rarely made close outside friendships with anyone, and became companions who played and worked together.

As the hands of time moved on, the family was becoming more and more inventive and mechanically minded. Lorin actually invented, patented, and put an improved hay press on the market. Wilbur was four years older than Orville, and, of course, a few years ahead of him in school. Also Wilbur was more interested in his studies. He liked to study and read good books.

In their home the Wright family had a library of over two

thousand volumes, books they had accumulated over a number of years. Susan, their mother, had always encouraged and helped her children to read and study. Most of the family were more interested in mechanical books and technical things. They all studied and worked together until they became extremely close companions, with a strong affection for one another. In this way it was easier for their mother to keep them home together when their father's duties took him from place to place.

Wilbur had blue eyes, thin brown hair, and a pale complexion. He was somewhat distant, had very little to say, and made but few friends. Orville became more friendly as the time went on. His hair was dark brown, and his eyes were also blue. Like his brother Wilbur, he was somewhat skinny but not as strongly built.

Reverend Wright and his wife were amazed at the two boys and their work as they grew into manhood. They made kites and other things while both parents advised them, always eager to help them develop any ideas or talents that interested them. In this way they shared each other's problems as they went along.

The two older boys, Reuchlin and Lorin, were now married. They had moved away and established homes of their own.

The Wright family lived on the west side of town in Dayton, on Hawthorn Street. Edward Sines, a boy everyone called Ed, lived in the same street and was the closest friend the Wright boys had. But Wilbur and Orville did not have much time for friends. They were always busy in school, reading, carving wood into towel racks, puzzles, and many useful things for their mother. Evenings, after supper the family gathered around and read magazine articles and newspaper stories about the various experiments being made all over the world. All five of them would discuss with great enthusiasm the accounts of the explorers, and the possibility of their chances with some unknown venture in the near future.

Then one afternoon, in late autumn, their father came home. He walked through the living room of their home on Hawthorn Street, with something covered up so no one could possibly see it. Up jumped Wilbur and Orville. "What is it, Father? Please, Father, what is it?"

"Something for you boys. Watch out." Their father opened

138

his hands, and a shiny object leaped into the air. It flew and soared, whirling as it rose higher toward the ceiling, fluttered as it crossed the room, then sank slowly to the floor.

Father Wright was very pleased with the way the boys responded to the demonstration of the little machine. "You see, boys," said Father, "it has two little fans that whirl around because of the rubber bands that are twisted tight. The frame was made out of bamboo and cork, and the rest of paper. This made the toy machine light, so the whirling fans were able to keep it up in the air as it turned very fast while the rubber band was unwinding to its normal position. It is called a helicopter."

For the next two weeks the boys were busy flying and watching their new toy. This helped to keep them out of trouble. They were like any normal boys, always getting into mischief, if nothing else, shooting at their neighbor's pets with pebbles in their slingshots. No doubt about it, ideas about flying must have been running through their minds as they watched the toy helicopter going up and down, under such a strain that in no time at all it was torn to bits.

Now Wilbur and Orville began to watch with amazement the birds, crows, and buzzards sail through the air overhead on a windy day. They were astonished at the way their wings supported them. Soon the boys were making toys of different shapes out of paper and sailing them through the air across the living room. They made kites and flew them against the wind, almost out of sight, high in the air as far as their balls of twine would allow them. They felt the wind pressure against the face of the kite as they slowly pulled it back to earth.

The boys were now growing up, becoming young men. Orville and Wilbur earned most of their spending money by making and selling toys, such as kites, always dividing the profit with their sister, Katharine. At seventeen, Wilbur quit high school in Richmond without graduating. His father had been editor of a church paper called *The Richmond Star*.

In 1884, when the family had once again settled down in their homestead on Hawthorn Street, Wilbur and Orville went back to working enthusiastically with their tools. Again they carved and engraved many decorative and serviceable creations of wood and sold them for use in a home, things such as towel racks, curtain rods, bookcases, and many other useful objects. Their mother sat watching as she knitted or darned the family clothes.

Many nights when the children slept, and Reverend Wright was away, Susan knelt by the window close to the bedside, her face turned toward heaven, while the bright stars sparkled like diamonds among the heavenly planets, twinkling far above Mars, Mercury, Venus, Jupiter or Saturn. As she knelt, starlight reflected on her pale tense face while she prayed for her family and talked with God. The night seemed to go quietly from her as she sank softly into vague distance, rest, and slumber.

She was a good mother. Although her heart was heavy she managed to conceal it. Tonight, as she lay on her pillow, memories of the past lived again in her mind, Susan had tuberculosis. Back in those days, the proper treatment for such a disease was unknown to mankind. She knew that she was living out her last days.

On July 4, 1889, she called the family to her bedside. While they were praying together, she left them with a smile on her lovely face. She had left them with skilled hands and minds she had trained from childhood to young manhood.

There is no limit to the hopes and understanding which a faithful, loving mother has for her family. If only it had been possible for her to look into the future, and if she could have visioned her two sons standing at the side of the President of the United States, or walking with the King of England! This was not to be, she had died in peace.

At the time of her mother's death, Katharine was only fifteen years old, Wilbur twenty-two, and Orville eighteen. The three were to become inseparable through the years. Although no credit was ever given to Katharine, she was a faithful silent partner to her brothers during their experimental years with their invention. Neither Orville nor Wilbur finished high school.

The two brothers started a printing press, and did job printing. Then, in 1892, they added a bicycle repair shop to their line of business. The sign above the modest shop in the two-story brick building at number 1127 West Third Street read "Wright Cycle Co." Here their business grew, and they soon became well known. Parts were ordered and assembled, and the bicycles were rugged and dependable. They sold some at nearly ninety dollars each.

Their success with the bicycle shop put their job printing

on the side. Ed Sines, their boyhood playmate, bought the printing business from them two years later.

Wilbur and Orville kept reading about a German by the name of Otto Lilienthal, an aeronautical inventor, who tried to fly with self-made wings by jumping off cliffs and tall buildings. The air pressure under the wings held him up for a short jump; but in 1896, he jumped one time too many and was killed. Thousands of people thought he was a fool to even try to fly.

In and behind their bicycle shop was where the Orville brothers began to create their airplane. Katharine, at the age of fifteen, tried hard to take their mother's place in the family. She washed the family clothes, cooked, sewed, and helped Wilbur and Orville with their problems. Meanwhile, the boys read everything that was available on flying. After an exhausting and difficult long day at the bicycle shop, they went straight home. No parties for them, they read, talked, and then off to bed.

The following May, 1899, the brothers obtained pamphlets from the Smithsonian Institution, *The Aeronautical Annuals of 1895 to 1897*, by James Means. They also read about other experiments on flying, and their interest grew stronger. They studied the failures and deaths of others who had tried to fly.

The disasters and difficulty of getting started was adding to their troubles, but this only encourage them. On July 22, 1899, Wilbur twisted an empty paper box in the shape of wings. The boys tested it, and were surprised to see it fly through the air.

Later, behind their bicycle shop, they fixed another workshop where they built so-called gliders, and conducted an epochal research in aerodynamics by means of their wind tunnel. Here a model was first made out of bamboo. It was a small biplane glider with threads to brace its parts together, and it worked.

Then a box five-foot wide and thirteen inches deep with curved surface and open sides was made. It was held in the air by cords. This was in August 1899, when Wilbur tried out this peculiar-looking box. It flew like a kite, with the help of a few small boys on Seminary Hill, about a mile from his home.

Wilbur was now thirty-two years old. The next step was to make a glider that would carry a man. After many attempts, the glider was finished. Then he wrote the U.S. Weather Bureau, and asked for a suitable place to test the glider.

A few days later he received a personal letter from the United

States Department of Agriculture, Weather Bureau, Office of the Observer, dated August 16, 1900. In the letter they advised the Wright brothers to go to Kitty Hawk, North Carolina, because there a steady and dependable wind flows mostly from the north and northeast during the months of September and October. Also they were advised to take along tents to live in because there was no place to stay. Transportation would be by sailboat from Elizabeth City, North Carolina, to Roanoke Island, then across Roanoke Sound to the beach at Kitty Hawk.

Here nature provided a suitable place for their glider experiment. Sand hills for the takeoff, steady winds, and soft sand for landing. The winds blew steady along the Atlantic Coast up to twenty-five miles an hour. What more could they want? They were very pleased with the report.

All through the spring and summer the boys worked continuously and untiringly on their glider. Wooden strips were soaked and used for the ribs; struts were shaped and fitted with movable joints, so that wires pulled over small pulleys might form a warp for the wing structure; and sateen fabric was bought for the wing covering. But they did not assemble the glider in Dayton. They planned to get some long, slender, strong sticks for the frame at Kitty Hawk.

Wilbur and Orville discussed the coming adventure in a deliberate fashion, with their sister Katharine offering varying opinions. Finally Orville agreed to stay and keep the bicycle shop open for business, while Wilbur went to Kitty Hawk.

On September 2, 1900, Wilbur started out alone with the materials and a camping outfit. After what seemed to be a cross-country journey, he finally arrived at Norfolk, Virginia. Here he was told that it was a whole day's trip (about sixty miles) to reach Elizabeth City, North Carolina. It seemed that no one at Norfolk had ever heard of such a place as Kitty Hawk. But Wilbur loaded his boxes into a coach on the old Norfolk & Southern Railroad. He didn't trust anyone to do this, and made sure that nothing had been misplaced or left behind.

As he sat there on the hard, oval, leather-covered iron seat the train began to move ahead as black smoke poured violently from the engine stack and covered the entire train. Her whistle screamed, and she huffed and puffed as she set in motion this huge mass of steel. On she rolled down the track, stopping at every little hamlet, to take on or put off passengers, mail, and freight. The sun rose higher in the sky, and Wilbur began to feel uncomfortable in the heat that came through the large, thick, plate-glass window; but he did not grumble.

Soon he began to respond to the thought of his ambition. He was taking his secret into a limitless abode of silence and desolation, where he could be alone with it. He had almost forgotten the reeling and rocking of the Old Iron Horse, as he mentally retraced his weary steps back to Dayton, Ohio, from where he had started.

The screaming whistle gave warning for the next stop, and brought him back from his lonely thoughts. Wilbur was a mild, gentle, silent kind of man, yet beneath his silence he seemed to be well occupied. To him, this seemed to be a rather wild and strange country.

He rose to his feet and began pacing to and fro in the aisle to stretch his aching bones, watching the weird and mystic shadows the moving train cast on the ground as it went rumbling around the bend.

After many forebearing and calmly tolerant hours, the Iron Horse crossed the Virginia stateline into North Carolina. The next stop, which was about two miles through the woods and reed patches, would be Moyock. Heat from the September sun bore down and could not pass unnoticed. Wilbur stepped off the train for a few moments to stretch his arms and legs. He marveled at the intense, eager interest these people showed while the train stood huffing and puffing.

Suddenly something began to stir in his veins, driven there by life's mysterious and remorseless motive, that some day there would be an awakening. Men and young boys sat in silver-trimmed leather saddles on restless horses. An old general store housed the furnishings for the whole neighborhood, along with a small space in the front of the store for the post office. Horses and buggies were tied to a hitching post and waiting in front of the store. A few clustered houses and shelters, along with a small saloon, made up the entire village.

Black smoke soared in the air, the whistle blew a screaming sound, and the train was again moving through more woods and low-spreading green bushes and reeds which grew alongside the tracks. Then on across open fields, with corn stalks waving

143

in the wind, heads slightly bowed, and turning brown in the hot September sun. All were left behind, after making stops at Snowden, Shawboro, Belcross, and Camden, which were only a few miles apart. At Camden Station the train stopped for a few moments. Wilbur was lost in another world, wondering whether this dream of his would ever come true.

Only time and fate would tell.

Across the aisle from Wilbur sat a very beautiful young woman (later to be identified as the lovely, graceful Nellie Cropsey, who lived on Riverside Avenue, in Elizabeth City, North Carolina. Little did she know that she was to be murdered by her lover in a matter of days).

The hands of time went on and at last the train pulled to a stop at the depot in Elizabeth City, North Carolina, only a few steps away from a horse and buggy taxi. Wilbur lost no time. In a few minutes all his boxes, which were arousing much attention at the station, were on their way toward the docks about one mile away. It was quite a load for the old horse to pull, and the buggy wheels popped and slapped as they ran out of one hole into another, down the dusty dirt Main Street that led from the depot to the waterfront. But at last the buggy pulled to a stop, only a few steps from the long warehouse which ran along the waterfront docks.

Wilbur paid the buggy driver fifty cents for his services. The sun was now low, shadows from the buildings hovered on the ground. People stopped to stare at Wilbur and his boxes. Freight trains stood on the tracks near the dock sheds, while neighbors' dogs bayed and prowled around the strange-looking black beast on the tracks that was coughing and puffing.

On this September 9, 1900, in Elizabeth City, North Carolina, Wilbur began talking with different people about Kitty Hawk. But they had never heard of the place. He walked a short distance from the train to the dock sheds, and talked to more people. By now he was beginning to wonder, as he walked through the long freight sheds and across the dock to the other side at the water's edge. Here he stopped and looked out across the river.

At this particular place, the river was narrow, not more than a thousand feet from the docks to the other side. The water was a dark, reddish-brown. (It received its color from the juniper and cypress swamps that drain into the river.) It was not like

144

the clear lakes, streams, and rivers that Wilbur had seen else-where.

On the other side of this narrow part of the Pasquotank River, across the channel, on the mud flats, he noticed a small one-mast sailing schooner lying at anchor. A man was rowing a skiff away from the schooner toward the dock where Wilbur stood. In a few minutes the man threw a small rope to him. Wilbur held the rope taut and steady the man climbed up on the dock.

"I am Captain Israel Perry. And who might you be?"

This was what seemed to be Wilbur's last chance, and he answered, "I am Wilbur Wright, from Dayton, Ohio. Have you ever heard of a place called Kitty Hawk, and could you tell me how I might get there?"

A somewhat surprised smile covered Captain Perry's tanned face. "Yes," he answered. "I am a native of Kitty Hawk, but now I live aboard that little flat-bottomed schooner you see off there. It has been my home now for some time."

Earlier, Wilbur had learned that a boat by the name of *Hattie Creef* made two trips weekly from Roanoke Island to Elizabeth City, but had left the docks at Elizabeth City about three hours before he arrived on the train. Wilbur did not want to wait; he was eager to get to his destination and begin experimenting with his glider.

After some discussion, Captain Perry agreed to take him and his boxes to Kitty Hawk. Soon some of the boxes were loaded into the little skiff and on their way to the sailboat that bobbed about in the light breeze. As Captain Perry rowed away from the wharf, Wilbur noticed that the skiff was leaking and he jokingly asked if it was safe. Captain Perry assured him that it was even safer than his sailboat.

Naturally this did not impress Wilbur. But rather than wait another week, he decided to stick to his agreement and go all the way. Back and forth they went for the rest of the boxes, then Wilbur climbed aboard the dirty little sailboat. Captain Perry tied the skiff to the stern of his floating home, and set sail down the Pasquotank River.

Toward the middle of the day a storm began to make up. Strong headwinds started to whip the sail, causing the small boat to pitch and roll. Later, the storm grew worse; and finally they were forced to search for a haven in North River. Here they anchored to wait for calmer weather.

It was now late in the afternoon. Black clouds had become darker and hung low. This made it seem later in the day than it was. Wilbur was a bit hungry, and wondered what Captain Perry was having for supper.

The galley was small. Captain Perry, half bent, managed to get through the door and began to mush up some food. Wilbur waited on deck. Sitting on an old long wooden box, he watched the storm, while scattered large drops of cool soft rain began to fall.

A few moments later, Wilbur rose and made his way across the uneven boards on deck to the entrance of the galley. The small sliding door that led down to the galley was open. Overhead, a round flat-bottomed rusty kerosene lantern, fastened to one of the unfinished beams, and smoked brown from the stove on which Captain Perry had cooked for many years, swung slowly with the motion of the little schooner as it rolled with the waves.

Bent over the cast-iron stove, Captain Perry was warming some sort of hash. He did not see Wilbur, who was quietly viewing the greasy dense galley. Wilbur wondered what kind of excuse to use for not eating. Then, without making any noise, he turned and silently crept up the steep and narrow old steps.

Back on deck, Wilbur opened his suitcase, hoping to find a miracle—and he found it. His sister Katharine had slipped a jar of homemade jelly under some of his clothes, just before he left home, back in Dayton, Ohio. This was a great relief. When supper was called, he politely told Captain Perry that he was not feeling well and would eat a little home-cooked jelly for his meal.

After this jelly "supper," without any bread, he was stlil hungry but didn't dare let it be known. While the storm raged outside, they sat in the smelly cabin talking and listening to the roar of the wind and rain driving against the cabin, causing the port holes to leak, with Captain Perry doing most of the talking.

Wilbur's thoughts were far away while they prepared to retire for the night. Captain Perry seemed to rest well despite the storm, and snored like a lion throughout the night. But Wilbur slept very little, and was mighty uncomfortable; he was not used to a bed rolling.

At daybreak it was dark and gloomy, and the storm raged on. Around one o'clock in the afternoon, the wind weakened, and clouds were breaking up and floating away. Then the rain stopped, the wind fell, the sun shone briefly through the openings in the clouds, and a light steady breeze blew from the southwest.

Soon the sail was up, and Wilbur took his usual seat aft on the wooden box. Captain Perry took the wheel, and the schooner started moving down the river and toward Kitty Hawk. The small boat exposed them to the direct heat of the September sun as they sailed on and into the Albemarle Sound, toward a place set aside from other parts of the Outer Banks, and the mainland, because of poor transportation and communication.

About 9:30 that night, they sailed into Kitty Hawk Bay. There the boat was anchored for the night. The little store at the shore end of the wharf was dark. A dim yellow light from an oil lamp showed through the window of a small fishing camp along the shore. It was too late to travel any further at night, so Wilbur stayed aboard the schooner until the next morning.

Captain Perry was still snoring at daybreak, when Wilbur rose from his bunk after a sleepless night. He had not rested well, and was beginning to feel the wear and tear of the trip during the past forty-eight hours, and trying to live on that jar of homemade jelly.

As a light streak began to arc the sky in the east along the horizon, Wilbur strolled up the little wharf and toward the shore. He met a young boy whose name was Elijah Baum. The boy was eager to show Wilbur where Captain Bill Tate lived, and after walking with him about a quarter of a mile, they reached his home. The date was September 11.

The Tates were very friendly. Wilbur received a warm welcome, and was just in time for breakfast. Never in all his life had ham and eggs ever tasted so good, along with hot biscuits, and yaupon. It almost made him forget the sore back he had acquired from lying on the hard deck of the sailboat. His arms still ached from grasping the sides of the schooner as it rolled and pitched during the wind and rain storm.

147

He had told the Tates about his forthcoming experiment, and they wanted to help.

Mrs. Addie Tate helped Wilbur with his sateen cloth. She used her foot-treadle type, Kenwood sewing machine to make the covering for the glider frame. Then all the materials and parts needed to assemble the glider were uncrated and carefully examined.

Back home at Number 7, Hawthorn Street, in Dayton, Ohio, his sister Katharine was very busy, keeping the home fires burning, still trying hard to take the place of their beloved mother, while Orville spent most of his time at the bicycle shop, and kept the business going in the two-story brick building at 1127 West Third Street.

In the next few days, Wilbur was very active. He went about his work in deep thought, while waiting, according to plan, for his brother Orville to join him at Kitty Hawk. Many afternoons Wilbur would stroll leisurely across the windblown sand ridges, through the tall scattered beach grass, feeling the steady pressure of the wind against his lean suntanned face, as he searched for a high sand hill suitable for his experiments with his glider.

On September 24, 1900, Orville Wright departed from his home in Dayton, Ohio, to join his brother at Kitty Hawk, hoping not to experience the same discomforts that Wilbur had in reaching Kitty Hawk from Elizabeth City.

Meanwhile, on September 15, 1900, the *Hattie Creef* began to make daily runs from Manns Harbor and Manteo to Elizabeth City, returning on the same day, making it more convenient for people along the Outer Banks.

On September 28, 1900, around 5:30 P.M., the old Norfolk & Southern Iron Horse came to a stop with a screeching sound, belching clouds of black smoke from her smokestack. Being informed earlier by mail about the traveling conditions and connections made it easier for Orville. Horses hitched to fancy black buggies with red wheels stood tied to the long hitching rail near the depot.

Without knowing who his passenger was, Henry Dawson carried Orville and his luggage, by horse and buggy, over the rough road and down the dusty street to the Hotel Arlington on Water Street. Tired from the long journey, Orville retired early for a long and comfortable night's sleep.

148

At eleven o'clock, next morning, Orville anxiously awaited the arrival of the *Hattie Creef*. He stood on the dock and gazed up and down the river, watching the busy little riverboats moving about in the harbor.

Later in the day, no questions were asked when Orville stepped aboard the *Hattie Creef* and paid his fare, one dollar and twenty-five cents, from Elizabeth City to Kitty Hawk. He was more than pleased with the comfort, the beautiful scenery, and delicious meals he enjoyed aboard. Orville personally thanked Captain Johnson as he left the boat at Kitty Hawk Bay, where he was met by his brother Wilbur and Captain Bill Tate. He had completed the eight-hundred-mile journey from Dayton, Ohio.

The sateen was now ready. With help of Wilbur's, it had been sewn into covers by Mrs. Addie Tate. Captain Tate helped the boys load their tent, the sateen covers, and other parts of the glider, into the cart. Soon they were moving over the windblown crest, a sea of sand and beach grass, passing clumps of low scattered bushes for a distance of five or six miles south of Kitty Hawk village to Kill Devil Hill. Here the Wright brothers set up their tent, and began assembling their first glider.

Where the north and northeast winds blew a strong, steady breeze, the area offered a soft landing in the sand for their glider, and here also were high and steep sand hills, free from trees or shrubs; all was perfect for carrying out their experiments. There was a feeling of fall in the air as the sun blazed down on this quiet, lonely spot, and a strong steady wind blew out of the north across the high, bleak, naked sand hills.

The cost of their first glider had been surprisingly small; not more than twenty-one dollars. A few weeks later, when the flight test was to be made, Orville held the glider up off the ground, while Wilbur ran ahead pulling it along with a rope like a kite. A sudden gust of wind caught under the wings, took the glider into the air, then pitched it forward and to the ground, breaking it to pieces.

Disappointed, of course; but they had learned one thing: that it *could* be done. They learned that the sateen cloth was too porous, full of tiny holes through which the air could flow too easily.

A few days later, before returning to their home in Dayton, Ohio, Wilbur gave the sateen to Mrs. Tate to make dresses for

149

her two little girls, Irene and Pauline. (Today the girls still have the sateen dresses in their possession as a keepsake.)

This time, traveling light, they were taken by Harris Midgett from Kitty Hawk to Elizabeth City in his small sailboat, where they boarded the Norfolk & Southern train for home.

Back at their bicycle shop in Ohio, many more experiments were carried out in the wind tunnel. Katharine was very excited over the progress her brothers were making and, to help in their experiments, gave them all the money she could spare while teaching school. She was well educated, and their silent partner in many ways.

For the next five or six months, Wilbur and Orville spent long hours working in their bicycle shop, and trying many experiments with their gliders as the hands of time moved on. They had no entertainment, and saved all the money that was possible in order to return to far-away Kitty Hawk and to the high bare-sand hills at Kill Devil Hill along the Outer Banks of North Carolina.

CHAPTER FOURTEEN

Honeymoon Hotel, Room No. 213

Meanwhile, the faithful *Hattie Creef* and her crew had continued making daily runs from Manteo, Manns Harbor, Nags Head, and Kitty Hawk to Elizabeth City, leaving at 5:00 A.M. and returning the same day, usually around 6:00 P.M., when the weather was normal.

On June 10, 1901, at Manteo, Captain Martin Johnson smiled and bowed as Gloria Midgette and Jimson Wise, stepped happily aboard the *Hattie Creef* at five o'clock in the early morning hours, along with other passengers enroute to Elizabeth City, to become husband and wife before returning to the historical island.

Captain Johnson was a great kidder. He enjoyed teasing young lovers, especially these beautiful native girls who were in love. Slowly the boat moved away from the dock and was soon out in the middle of Albemarle Sound, sailing with a strong southwest wind against her sails.

Like so many young couples in love, and preferring to be alone, Gloria and Jim sat near the bow in the shade of the tall impressive mast that held the weight of the mainsail. They pretended to be watching the small boats fishing for white perch and croakers. But while they sat silently, hand in hand, their minds were far away.

Gloria's thoughts turned to the yesterdays when she had sat perched high on a sand hill on the beach. There on a clear day she could see many ships come and go along the beautiful horizon, watch the porpoise play in the sparkling turquoise blue Atlantic on which whitecaps rode the rolling, foaming waves to the very impressive shoreline along the seemingly endless stretch of lovely washed sand and pebbles.

She could still hear the distant steady rumble of the waves making a thunderous sound as they broke on the beach; the small hilly, irregular desert of yellow sand, and on past the patches of evergreen bushes and sea oats that provided life for the wild ponies which roamed the Outer Banks. She recalled sitting alone among the sand dunes near the surf, and dreaming in silence under the soft silvery light from the full moon overhead, better known along the Outer Banks as the "Carolina moon."

Suddenly Gloria thought of the striking contrast when, on dark stormy nights, something seems to creep out of the darkness from nowhere. Each night, out of the gloom, it fills the air with loneliness and terror of the past, along the Outer Banks, through the veil of centuries, where the many unsolved mysteries of North Carolina surpass all other parts of the state.

Jim called her attention to a school of jumping mullets, leaping one after another out of the water, glittering in the sunlight, off the starboard side. The *Hattie Creef* was now approaching Hospital Point, which projected out from the shore for a short distance into the river. She sailed up the Pasquotank River, and soon she was secured at the dock, her sails lowered and made fast to the mast.

Jim and Gloria strolled along the dirt street, for one block, to Water Street, unmindful of the magnificent gold and red sunset that blazed on the path before them and gradually sank behind the low, flat-top, wooden buildings, while long dark shadows crept across the street as the couple turned left at the corner of Water Street and Colonial Avenue.

On the opposite corner, directly across the street, Doctor McMullen's Drugstore, established in 1889, was busy with customers.

Jim and Gloria stopped about halfway in the block, at the hitch-rail in front of the Arlington Hotel. At the entrance, a small square marble slab set in bricks, dated 1891, bore the scars and wear from footprints placed there by the hands of time. This was a three-story, red-brick hotel, with long hallways, and a large dining room where one homemade wooden table, about twenty feet long, stood draped with a colorful tablecloth that reached almost to the clean shining floor.

Food on beautiful platters decorated the table from end to end, with ham, chicken, steaks, fish, oysters, and many other dishes fit for a king. Guests sat in high-back chairs, eating supper, as Gloria and Jim shyly entered to read the menu posted on the wall. Meals were thirty-five cents; eat all you wanted, what you wanted, and when you wanted it. Looking rather surprised, they quietly sat down near the end of the long table and began eating.

After the delicious meal, Jim and Gloria walked down the wide steps from the second floor to the street, stopping once again in front of the long hitching rail to look at the thoroughbred saddle horses which stood quietly resting, bearing silver-trimmed western saddles that sparkled in the candlelight from the lobby of the Hotel Arlington.

Walking slowly and turning at the next corner to the right, led them up Main Street on the dusty, rough sidewalk. One block away E. S. Chesson & Son displayed a sign over their clothing store, which had been established in 1900. Across the street, a sign read "Louis Selig," since 1882. In the same block on the corner was McCabe & Grice, established in 1898. Also The First & Citizens National Bank, opened in 1891. Two blocks away up Main Street, on the front of the Courthouse the date was 1882. (Jim Wilcox had been later tried there and found guilty of the murder of Nellie Cropsey.) Not far away was the Christ Episcopal Church, built in 1856. It extended from McMorrine Street to Fearing Street. Owen's Shoe Company had opened its doors for business in the spring of 1901.

There were no paved streets or sidewalks. Numerous people passed by, moving in both directions in this lively little riverboat town of Elizabeth City, chartered in 1793.

The world of 1900 is well within the memory of many living vigorous men and women. And yet, when they talk to us about this century's early days, it is as if they were from another planet.

Jim and Gloria strolled leisurely on. Gaslights lit the streets for the horses and buggies. There were no such things as electric refrigerators, few gas stoves, no airplanes, no radios, few telephones, and no miracle drugs. Diphtheria, typhoid fever, and whooping cough were dreaded diseases, often fatal to infants and older children.

Women were not allowed to vote. Labor unions were small and few; wages of one dollar and fifty cents a day were paid for hard labor. Children worked in coal mines twelve hours daily for thirty-five cents a day. Sugar was four cents a pound, butter could be bought for twenty-four cents a pound. A lady cashier could earn up to eight dollars per week, but some women earned as little as two dollars and fifty cents a week.

Although the telephone had been invented in 1876, it was little known, until the year 1900. It was not very important to the people of North Carolina. There were no ready-made bathing suits; cloth by the yard was purchased for the purpose, and after being hand-made the suits had the appearance of a dress. And when bathing, the women also wore a round cap with an elastic band. It resembled a dustcap. Swimsuits for the men were more like a nightgown. At the turn of the century, a pretty face was just about all a lady could show of herself. Modesty demanded that she hide her figure under yards of bulky petticoats and ruffles, which concealed the true shape of her bosom and extending well down to her ankles—except perhaps for only a discreet tantalizing glimpse.

At dusk, lamplighters climbed ladders to turn on the town's gaslights. In most small towns, yellow lights flickered from the kerosene oil lamps on the lamp posts along the rough, dusty and unpaved streets.

Gloria and Jim strolled up Main Street until they noticed a small rectangular board fastened to a tree that leaned toward the street. Twilight had faded, gloom closed in over the area. A dim yellow light from a well-trimmed wick inside a clear glass globe of a kerosene lantern that hung on a lamb, reflected on the sign. It read: Parson Jones. As she looked at it for a moment, Gloria's heart skipped a beat and she pressed her hand into Jim's. Then they climbed the porch steps together.

A few knocks, and soon an elderly and somewhat stooped man opened the heavy hand-carved mahogany door. With a warm smile he invited them into his home. Antique candlesticks held the candles that burned at each end of the decorative mantle carved from bird's-eye maple. A soft glow from the candles reflected in the large mirror over the mantle in this peaceful room. Large ancestral, lifelike pictures gazed at them.

For the next few minutes, Parson Jones thoroughly explained the obligatory responsibility of a man and his wife to each other, their respect to society, and their obligation to God, before he pronounced them man and wife, joining them together in the name of God as one flesh. It was a quiet, simple ceremony! exactly the way they both had wanted it to be.

154

After paying Parson Jones his fee of two dollars, the newlyweds were on their way. Dust rose from the hoofs of a horse and buggy that passed them. Odd hitching posts dotted the edge of the sidewalks, horses stood quietly resting, in front of the Pool Parlor on Colonial Avenue. Others were tied to hitching rails near a glass-front restaurant, and some patiently waited, without flinching, in front of a smoke-filled camouflaged saloon.

When the young couple returned to the hotel, a surprise party, given by the management, awaited them. It was a great success, with music, singing, and dancing until one o'clock. There were many useful gifts for the bride and her husband.

The desk clerk escorted Jim and his wife to the top floor, to a room with a large window that overlooked the Pasquotank River. A fancy white iron bed stood against the wall. One high-back drab chair filled the corner of the room. Wooden clothes hangers hung on a wooden peg near the end of a mirrored washstand that held a thick large washbowl, a pitcher of water, and towels were draped on a rack beneath the rectangular mirror. Below, twin doors opened in the middle, swinging out to each side, provided space for baggage. A rack fastened to the wall held a kerosene lamp that furnished the only light for the room.

In the long hallway a ten-gallon wooden keg, resting on a low table rack against the wall, was filled with ice water that could be drawn by turning the faucet either way near the bottom of the keg.

The lock clicked as their bedroom door closed. To them, moments later as they embraced each other, the rest of the world ceased to exist. Several beautiful nightgowns, received as gifts at the hotel party, were cast aside. Jim suddenly but gently flung Gloria's shapely curved body on the soft mattress, where they politely embraced each other. Moments later, silence filled the room. A light cool breeze that blew across the amber-colored water of the Pasquotank River crept quietly through the screen as the newlyweds slipped away into dreamland.

The next morning, through the open window a glorious stream of golden sunlight shone with a long slant on the bed. While Jim slept, Gloria lay in a horizontal position and watched the mysterious shadows of objects move slowly about the room on the wall, silent as morning clouds, while the sun rose higher in the sky.

155

A little later she sat in a chair near the window, her arms folded and resting on the window sill, looking out over the river. In the brilliant summer sunlight, she saw the white sails of the *Hattie Creef* as she passed Hospital Point, nearing the end of her journey. Gloria called to Jim as she turned away from the window, and began to dress. Soon a hardy breakfast was enjoyed by the newlyweds.

Jim could not help but admire his lovely wife as they left the hotel on their way to the dock to meet the *Hattie Creef*. Gloria was bareheaded, and her dark-brown hair hung in curls about her shoulders. Jade-green eyes reflected a burning passion, and her flexible, full-breasted, shapely figure displayed a beautiful woman.

When they reached the dock, the proud queen had been made fast to the piling. Everyone was beginning to depend on her; she had proved herself worthy of the responsibilities: carrying mail, passengers, freight, and making daily runs from Manns Harbor, Manteo, Nags Head, Kitty Hawk, and Elizabeth City. The only dependable connection between Roanoke Island and Elizabeth City, she played an important part in the development of transportation and communication between these isolated points along the Outer Banks of North Carolina.

Five days later, Jim and Gloria boarded the *Hattie Creef* at the dock in Elizabeth City, to return to Roanoke Island after an unforgettable honeymoon at the Hotel Arlington. Abreast of Camden Point, on their way back to their native island, the best pan mullets, eggbread, and hot coffee that could be cooked were served by Lee Dough while under full sail.

Guitars and mouth harps furnished the music for entertainment, and for the singing of spiritual hymns by all. Soon the schooner sailed passed Point Harbor, and they were in sight of this beautiful, historical island shrouded by mysteries. A welcome for the newlyweds soon began to fade away as passengers hurriedly walked toward their respective places.

George Washington Creef, Jr., was proud of the ship that he and his men had built. He also showed great pride and joy in the way Captain Martin Johnson and Lee Dough were successfully sailing the *Hattie Creef* on their schedule runs.

On July 14, 1901, Captain Johnson lowered the mainsail and slowly moved his ship toward her berth, making her fast to the dock at Elizabeth City. Another couple from the Outer Banks were here to be married, and to spend their honeymoon at Hotel Arlington.

Captain Johnson personally escorted them around the corner to the hotel. He introduced them to the manager as Marty Daniels and Mary Austin, soon to become man and wife. Before having dinner in the long dining hall, Marty helped her to a chair beside him. He respected a silence which he divined was full of a woman's deep emotion and beyond his interpretation.

Grandmother's quilting parties were rapidly becoming extinct. The *Hattie Creef* had paved a way to the outside world. Culture was becoming spiced with lively loose-jointed figures, and outfits decorated with multicolored designs, draped these bold beauties from a land of mystery.

After dinner, the young couple were on their way to see Parson Jones. When they arrived, a sign on his door read: "Out of Town. Attending a funeral. Will return at 8:00 P.M."

With time on their hands, they had an urge to explore this lively growing little town. They began to move about, while horse and buggies leisurely jogged down the uneven dusty streets.

Large, spreading trees along the way furnished shade from the mid-July sun. Many eye-catching sights were remembered. On they strolled. Soon a long string of small colorful sea shells, spaced with chainyberry-tree beads, dangled around Mary's lovely neck.

When the sun disappeared behind the trees, the pale afterglow remained in the sky after sunset and darkened with the merging of twilight into night. The streets were black and gloomy, but stars began to glimmer overhead. Suddenly Marty and Mary turned and walked in the direction of Parson Jones' home.

The sound of trotting horses broke the silence as night riders passed in the soft night wind, barely making a shadow while passing dim yellow lights that flickered on the lamp post at every corner of the unpaved streets.

When they arrived, Parson Jones gave them a very warm welcome. The quiet ceremony was soon completed, in the same lovely surroundings which Gloria and Jim had enjoyed. Then, arm in arm, they walked back to the hotel, this time to register as Mr. and Mrs. Marty Daniels.

While they had been away in the afternoon, the hotel manager busied himself with the same room which Jim and Gloria had occupied on their honeymoon in June. As the town clock in the courthouse tower on Main Street struck twelve, the manager showed them to their room. The night latch broke the silence when it clicked as the door closed behind them.

For the next few minutes, Marty and Mary shyly stared at the bright light of the lamp chimney. A full moon gradually rose in the east, spraying moonlight on the dancing little ripples on the surface of the Pasquotank River. Gloom from the dense cypress and pine trees growing along the shore made a black hidden shoreline in the moonlight.

As the bright cold moon rose higher in the sky, across the room moonbeams cast a light through the screen in the window. Mary blew out the oil lamp, and began to undress. Soon lust and desire for each other overpowered them as they hugged and kissed in the soft moonlight, and brought them great happiness.

From then on, the same room, No. 213, was reserved for married couples on their honeymoon. Along the Outer Banks, the Arlington soon became known as "Honeymoon Hotel." While the *Hattie Creef* sailed on and on, many young lovers continued to marry and honeymoon at the Hotel Arlington in Elizabeth City, North Carolina.

CHAPTER FIFTEEN

Unsolved Murder

In far away New York State, lived a family by the name of Cropsey. William Hardy Cropsey married Mary Vandelt Ryder. As the years passed, ten lovely children were born to William and his wife Mary.

The girls were Olive Cecelia, Ella Maud, Mary Gertrude, Caroline, Aletta, and Louisa. The four boys were Jerome, Frederick, William, and Andrew Douglas. Some of the children died when very young.

Mr. Cropsey was well known as a commission merchant, and they lived near the waterfront in the crowded section of Brooklyn. Mrs. Cropsey and the children wanted to move where they could be exempted from the discomforts of the door to door apartments, as well as the crowded streets and subways. The rattle and clanging of the elevated cars running on steel tracks overhead could be heard all day and most of the night.

After some lengthy family discussions around the dinner table, Mr. Cropsey decided to look for a change. He also knew that Brooklyn was no place to raise a large family. He knew from reliable sources that Northeastern North Carolina had a wonderful climate, and was a suitable and profitable place for dealing in potatoes and grain, and had many other advantages.

Mr. Cropsey came south alone. He soon located the Pasquotank County section, along the river in Elizabeth City, which he liked very much. He was amazed as he stood on the dock at the water's edge along the Pasquotank River, and carefully observed the possibilities in this region. Low, flat, dark, rich soil was excellent for growing crops. It was also a fine location for boating and fishing, as well as a great place for living.

Soon Mr. Cropsey was back in Brooklyn, New York, revealing to his wife Mary and the children what he had found out about this wonderful part of the country, and about its natural beauty. Without any delay, all belongings were quickly made ready for the journey, including Mr. Cropsey's walking canes, which were part of a well-dressed man's wardrobe, during and after the turn of the century. Mr. Cropsey was busy at the office advising his associates about the change he was making. The Cropseys were a prominent family. Mr. Cropsey was a buyer of grain and potatoes for commission merchants in New York.

On April 20, 1898, the Cropsey family arrived on the Norfolk & Southern Railroad train at the depot in Elizabeth City. Some of the children were small, but two daughters were old enough to have dates.

The Cropseys soon located a house on Riverside Avenue, where only a few scattered homes had been built many years before. There were no paved streets or sidewalks, but only dirt roads for horse-drawn carts and buggies. In this section, the roads were usually rough and dusty, except during rainy weather; and then they were muddy and full of holes.

(The house was located one and a half blocks from where the old Albemarle Hospital now stands and is presently known as the College of the Albemarle. It is a well known Junior College along the banks of the Pasquotank River, about two hundred feet from the river shore.)

It was a beautiful location for romantic lovers. The reddish-brown, amber-colored water washed the grayish-white sand along the shore where cypress knees push their way up above the surface of the dark water, and grow near the cypress trees in many decorative shapes and sizes. The beautiful Carolina full moons, and overhanging moss-draped trees growing at the river's edge add great beauty for the young at heart.

The house which the Cropseys found was (and still is) a wonderful old home. The interior consisted of eight spacious rooms with high walls, lively hallways, magnificent mantles, and lovely stairways. A decorative vestibule opened out on a sturdy porch that extended across the front, and partly around each side of this imposing dwelling. Large strong columns supporting the porch roof stood at attention, without budging, fighting the hands of time. Footworn steps led up from the grassy lawns stood ready and obedient for the purpose.

This two-story wood-frame mansion had a decorous clear glass front tower that adorned the front of the house at the top of the upper story, adjoining the dark-gray slate roof. It overlooked the

Pasquotank River, only about two hundred feet away. Many moon beams have sparkled and danced on the ripples made by gentle soft breezes that move across the river.

Although Mr. Cropsey was known to be a Yankee, and the embers from the fire kindled by the Civil War between the North and South were still burning, he and his family were liked by everyone. In a short time he became very successful, both socially and financially, in what was then a small coastal, or river-boat and farming town.

At that time Riverside Avenue was (and still is) considered the best and oldest residential section in the community. Many lively parties were enjoyed at the Cropsey home. All their six daughters were pretty, but Nellie, now almost seventeen, and Olive Cecelia, eighteen were the most attractive.

The Foremans, the Blades, and the Kramers of the younger generations soon found ways of being presented to the beautiful Cropsey girls. Nellie, or Nell as she was known to most, was only a nickname. Her real name was Ella Maud Cropsey, born to Mary and William Cropsey, in Brooklyn, New York, in 1882.

Nellie was sixteen years old when, in 1898, her family moved from Brooklyn to Elizabeth City, North Carolina. In Brooklyn, she had been going rather steady with a young man by the name of Willie Brooks. They had continued to keep in touch by corresponding.

During this time, James Wilcox met Nellie and fell in love with her. Almost every night Jim went to the Cropsey home to see her. Sometimes he brought along a friend of his, Roy Crawford, who was dating Ollie. At this time, Wilcox did not know about Nell's boy friend in Brooklyn.

Usually they all sat in the parlor, and sang songs while one of them played the piano. Bedtime was called at eleven o'clock. Then the music stopped, the soundwaves from their beautiful voices as they sang hymns of praise, slowly faded away, and the young men left for home.

According to reports from some of the older natives in Elizabeth City, Nellie was very beautiful, of the highest quality, and worshipped by all in the social surroundings; a young woman all artists and lovers always dream of but do not readily find. She was referred to as the "beautiful Nell Cropsey"; a well deserved, suitable title, according to the records, and the photographs which still exist today in the town in which she was mysteriously murdered.

Dark-brown curls hung impressively on her shoulders, when they were not tied back. Deep-blue eyes, glowing with intense emotional excitement and intelligence, added greatly to her shapely figure.

Jim Wilcox was the son of Thomas Wilcox, a former Pasquotank County sheriff, with whom Jim still lived. Jim was twenty-five years old, a short, stocky, hot-tempered man, and worked as a sawmill laborer.

Nell's father greatly disapproved of their courtship, and many times became extremely angry with her. Wilcox gave her virtually all his spare time, and loved her without doubt, for almost three years. One night Nell mentioned to her older sister Ollie, that she was getting impatient with Jim because of their long courtship, and that she had decided to marry her Brooklyn boy friend.

After a brief discussion, Nell reached a decision to fan a flame of jealousy by showing Jim that she could also be charming to other men. In this way she hoped to discourage him from coming to see her. The next day she began to flirt in a rather moderate manner with other acquaintances. This soon caused an argument, which ended with tears and expressions of regret.

Meanwhile, in some way the news leaked out about Nell's boy friend back in Brooklyn. Also of her intentions. It was never known how Wilcox discovered this secret. But on November 20, 1901, according to the record, Jim Wilcox called on Nellie as usual at her home.

Their love affair now was not going so well. When Jim walked into the parlor, Carrie Cropsey, Nell's cousin from New York, was visiting them and talking to a young man who lived in the neighborhood. Ollie and her beau, Roy, were also present. No one seemed to be in the mood for music or singing, so the conversation drifted as they sat in the parlor, and they soon became bored.

Jim Wilcox was unusually quiet, causing Ollie to wonder what was on his mind. Finally she asked him why he kept watching the clock on the mantle, but received only a casual glance without an answer. Around eleven o'clock Jim rose from his chair, and briefly remarked that he must be going.

As the story goes, Jim held the interior front door to the vestibule open a bit and in a low indistinct voice mumbled something about wanting to speak to Nell. She hesitated for a moment, then looked uncertainly at Ollie, who nodded her approval.

Nellie rose and walked slowly across the room toward the door, tall straight walls in the parlor echoed the sound of her footsteps. Out of the night, the eyes of death stared unnoticed through the partly closed door, where Jim Wilcox stood waiting. Nell closed the door behind her, never again to be seen alive.

At the Cropsey home, no one waited up for her. William and Mary Cropsey retired shortly after midnight, according to Ollie and Carrie. While Ollie's boy friend, Roy, was on his way home, Cousin Carrie and Ollie were snug in their beds. When the clock on the mantle began to strike one-thirty A.M., Ollie jumped out of bed and hurriedly tiptoed to Nell's bedroom.

In the gloomy darkness she reached out to touch Nell's pillow, only to find it cold and empty. Cautiously she walked down the winding stairs to the hallway that led to the vestibule, cold chills creeping over her body. After calling in every direction from the door that someone had left open, and hearing no answer but only the constant moaning of the wind as it blew through the large pine treetops, that stood between the house and the river, she closed the door and made her way back to her room. But could not sleep. She was afraid and lonely as time dragged by. Tick-tock—tick-tock—the clock on the mantle below in the parlor had an unusually loud sound and broke the dead silence that filled her room.

Suddenly the whistle at the sawmill blew, and their dog barked in a very excited manner as if someone was near the house. Ollie jumped out of bed and ran across the hall to her parents' bedroom. Mr. Cropsey dressed and hurried down the stairs to the back door, firmly holding his shotgun.

The thought of a thief, his daughter or Jim Wilcox wandering about in the wee hours of the morning, made him furious. But a thorough search of the grounds around the house turned up nothing.

Still no information about Nell.

The whole family became worried. Mr. Cropsey hurried over to the Wilcox residence, and pounded on the door. Jim's father, the ex-sheriff, answered, but stated that Jim had been home since midnight. Mr. Cropsey insisted on seeing Jim.

163

It took some effort to arouse Jim from a deep sleep. After hearing his story Mr. Cropsey returned home, worried and bewildered. Fear and anxiety began to grip the entire Cropsey household. Police Chief Henry Dawson was immediately notified. He came without delay to the Cropsey home, and searched the neighbors' homes, yards, and outbuildings. The river's edge was also searched for tracks along the shore. But there was no trace of Nellie, although the tide had risen and fallen since the night before.

Jim Wilcox was again questioned, and gave a step by step account of the happenings of the night before. He said that he left his home at 8:00 P.M. to take Nellie an umbrella that he had borrowed, also a picture of her that she had given him almost three years before; that he had not planned to stay, but Ollie insisted when he arrived. Jim admitted asking Nell to go out on the porch with him, and there he told her he was not coming back again. He said that she leaned against the porch column, her head on her folded arms, and began to cry. Then he asked her to stop crying and go to bed, but she refused. Moments later, Jim said, he told her he had to meet a man at Barne's Bar before it closed. At this, she told him to go. And he did.

During further questioning, Wilcox stated that he loved Nellie very much, always would, and that nothing could change it. He appeared to be very much disturbed. He also stated that after leaving Nellie, he had wandered down the rough dusty road and took a longer time than usual before going to Barne's Bar, where he had a glass or two of beer with a friend before going home and straight to bed.

Chief Henry Dawson checked out his story. The umbrella was found in the hallway rack at the Cropsey residence; he had had the beer at the barroom; but no picture was ever found. Chief Dawson decided to detain Wilcox until the case was thoroughly checked out.

Tension among friends was rapidly increasing. Before daybreak, on November 21, Jim Wilcox was placed behind bars in the Pasquotank County Jail on Pool Street, in the custody of Deputy Charles Reid. (This same old red-brick jail that still stands, built in 1889, is being used today in Eliazbeth City, North Carolina.)

Bloodhounds were used to follow the family trail from the front porch to the river, back and forth, but no evidence was found or any indication that Nellie had been to either place. Then a wide, long area of the river was dragged; more houses were searched, not only in town, but in all adjoining counties. Still no clue.

Angry feelings among the people everywhere ran higher against Jim Wilcox. He was questioned over and over, hour after hour, and it was found that he did not reach his home until after 1:30 A.M., on the night of November 20; and that he had also had a blackjack, which he had boastfully shown to his friends on the same night.

News of Nellie's disappearance became widely known. Letters from many directions were received by the Cropsey family. Some stated that they had seen the "Beautiful Nellie Cropsey" and had talked with her the day before. These letters brought no relief to this distressed, almost crazed sleepless family.

Then, on December 24, a letter postmraked "Utica, New York," came in the mail. It gave information relating to the events of the night on November 20. The writer revealed that Nellie had been dazed by a blow on the head with a blunt instrument, that her body had been carried to the river, placed in a skiff, and rowed out a short distance from the shore, dead or unconscious, where she was dumped into the river in deep water. The letter from Utica, New York, included a detailed diagram where the body could be found, and the spot marked. A search for the letter was made later, but it could not be found.

Every night Nell's heartsick, sorrowful mother would go down to the river to watch and search along the shore in hopes of finding her daughter. There seemed to be times when the family would build strong hopes that she was still alive, only to have them fade away. Then they drifted back into the channel of loneliness and despair.

After the morning chores were finished, Mary climbed the winding stairway and worked her way up to the tower that overlooked the peaceful Pasquotank River. Here she sat on a low wooden stool and watched in silence, hoping to unravel the mysterious disappearance of her lovely daughter.

Today her heart was extremely heavy, tears rolled down her tense face through misty eyes as she watched the *Hattie Creef* pass by in the channel not far from the shore, nearing the end of her journey, and loaded as usual with passengers, freight, and mail. Minutes later she tied up near the well known Hotel Arlington, alongside the Nathan Grandy Dock.

Another day was ending. The hands of time had left another day behind them. The sun slowly sank behind the buildings in this emotionally aroused, growing little town. Red and gold shafts of sunlight cast a brilliant, shimmering glare across the water. Nightfall soon began to settle over this troubled area.

Quietly Mary descended to the entrance hallway, then went through the living room, and on to the kitchen where supper was prepared for the family. She sat down to eat, but her appetite was gone. Tonight the moon was full, and cast bright beams through the openings in the trees on the front porch. Mary stood idly in the doorway. The tired and weary mother walked across the narrow boards to the steps that led to the worn path under the trees to the road, then on to the river shore about two hundred feet away, to watch unceasingly.

What little sleep she'd had lately had been harassed by strange dreams, finally to awake wet with cold sweat. Tonight she was fully entranced by her thoughts. She failed to see the long, dark shadows of the cypress trees along the shore, and on the water at the river's edge, as they moved slowly and became shorter as the full moon rose higher and higher in the sky.

The gentle west wind had lulled at sunset; the vast area of small ripples on the surface of the river had vanished and left it undisturbed. Loneliness filled the air, and Mary shivered from the chill of the night and drew her cloak firmly around her shoulders.

Soon the clock in the tower on Main Street struck twelve. Overhead, the moon shove brightly down on the calm, silent Pasquotank River. Mary wept bitterly at times, while she waited.

Suddenly Mrs. Cropsey saw something white floating on the moonlit water. A strange weak feeling began creeping over her tired body as she turned and quickly went for help.

A neighbor rowed out in a skiff, and brought the body of "Beautiful Nellie Cropsey" ashore.

It was amazing how well the icy amber-colored water in the river had preserved her body for thirty-seven days. Now all hopes of seeing her alive had perished.

The news traveled swiftly, and soon a lynching party was formed. Mob after mob of angry people crowded around the

166

jail, swinging a rope, and screaming to hang Wilcox from the nearest tree. Tremendous excitement seized the area in and around Elizabeth City on this horrible night of December 27, 1901.

Soon uncontrollable groups refused to move away from the jail, and stood shouting threats to go on with the lynching. Mr. Cropsey refused to have anything to do with the mob. The situation was getting out of control. In contrast to the excitement, Wilcox remained cool and collected. But Sheriff Grandy called Governor Charles B. Aycock for help. Governor Aycock immediately sent the Naval Reserves to the jail. The angry mobs slowly but stubbornly moved away, shouting as they left.

All loose ends were pulled together, and circumstantial evidence pointed its finger at Jim Wilcox. The motive that he was about to be jilted by this beautiful woman, the blackjack that he had carried, and when two days before the murder he tried to get Nellie and Ollie to go sailing down the river with him by force all led to Wilcox facing a charge of murder.

Irving Fearing and two physicians entered in their death report that Nellie Cropsey had died from a blow on the left temple and by drowning. This report led to a discussion in which there was disagreement for some time. Finally the coroner changed his report, and stated that no water had been found in the lungs of the dead girl.

Then the physicians agreed that the blow on the temple, by a round instrument something like a blackjack, was the cause of her death. No other marks of violence on her body were found.

The trial got under way on March 14, 1902, with Judge A. Jones presiding. The jury was selected after several days of shuffling. George Ward was the solicitor. He told the jury that Wilcox had used the special combination of circumstances, which were favorable for the purpose of killing Nellie Cropsey on the night of November 20, 1901.

Because of the confusion in the death report, Ward continued to cross-examine the physicians on the witness stand. Through the medical testimony, Ward tried to show the jury that the girl did not die from drowning, but that she was dead or dying before being thrown into the Pasquotank River.

The trial lasted for eight days, and the testimony ended with the statement that she did not drown, and that death was caused by a hard blow on the left temple.

In summing up the facts to the jury, Solicitor George W. Ward stated that "only one man" could tell, and Jim Wilcox was the man. That if the trees could talk, if the wind and stars could talk, they could tell, but Wilcox was the only human being who could tell—but he remained cool and quiet.

Defense Attorney E. F. Adylett rose to begin his vigorous attack, while the judge watched in amazement as large crowds of angry spectators started leaving the courtroom. As Lawyer Aydlett started charging the jury, a false fire alarm was turned in.

Thirty days went by, before the jury could decide on a verdict. Meanwhile the town had come to a halt. People lingered all day, some missed their meals, cursed and excited others around them, expressing their dissatisfaction over the delay. Then after basing the verdict on circumstantial evidence only, and on the fact that Wilcox was the last person to have seen Nellie Cropsey alive, at 10:10 P.M. on March 22, the courthouse bell rang out to announce the decision. The same bell hangs silent in the belfry today.

By the dim flickering lights of the oil lamps set in small iron hoop-shaped racks on the sides of the high walls, Judge Jones asked Wilcox to rise. Calm but pale, he rose and heard his death sentence.

Later he was granted a new trial at Hertford, a small town eighteen miles west of Elizabeth City, in Perquimins County, North Carolina. This time he was charged with second-degree murder. The trial was short. He was quickly found guilty, and sentenced to life imprisonment at hard labor.

At neither trial did Jim Wilcox take the witness stand in his defense and deny the murder. He was immediately sent to the State Penitentiary, where he served behind prison walls until December 20, 1920.

Wilcox was a short, stocky man, with a fiery quick temper, and wore a mustache. While in prison, he whittled and carved three walking canes out of wood. On top of one of the canes, at the curve where the hand fits, he carved an apple. On another cane he carved a snake, and on the third cane at the top on the curve he carved a house with a round roof. All resembled the work

168

of a person who was very skillful or highly trained for this special field.

At that time, Locke Craig, from Buncombe County, was Governor of North Carolina from 1913 to 1917. During his term in office, Wilcox wrote to him asking to be pardoned from the State Penitentiary. But Governor Craig refused.

In 1917, Thomas W. Bickett, from Franklin County was elected Governor, and served through 1921. A few days before December 20, 1920, Wilcox talked with the warden at the prison, and asked to see Governor Bickett. Soon a meeting was arranged.

Before leaving, Governor Bickett stated that he was to visit a prison camp near the Blue Ridge Mountains where Jim Wilcox was confined, and that he had planned to talk with him. After talking with Wilcox, at first Governor Bickett also refused to grant him a pardon. But later he reviewed the conversation, and finally gave Wilcox his freedom.

Neither of the Governors, according to the record, could understand why Jim Wilcox did not take the witness stand to deny his guilt and offer a defense on his own behalf. Evidently Governor Bickett was convinced that Wilcox did not kill Nellie Cropsey as charged, when he set him free. Did Governor Bickett really discover the true story of the murder? Some people believe that he did. But no one will ever know what Wilcox told Governor Bickett about the murder, or what really did happen on that November night in 1901, because both men are dead. What was revealed, or how much, still remains a secret. Nothing was ever placed on record.

On Christmas Eve, December 24, 1920, Jim Wilcox stepped from the train when it stopped at the depot in Elizabeth City. He was not the young lover of eighteen years ago, on trial for his life, but a much older and different person in mind, body, and soul.

After he was released from prison, for about two years Wilcox worked as maintenance man for the Fire Department in Elizabeth City. Then he began to live a secluded, solitary life, feeling that no one wanted him around. Part of the time he lived with his sister, Mrs. Edward Ferebee, on Dyer Street.

Several times he was seen walking alone, past the former Cropsey residence on Riverside Avenue. Although the Cropseys had been gone since 1903, without a doubt, as Wilcox walked slowly by the house, memories of the past came to life again.

In 1903, Mr. Edward Outlaw, a native of Bertie County, North Carolina, bought the former Cropsey home and moved his family there.

As the hands of time moved on, Jim became very lonely and could be seen hanging around the livery stables on the corner of Poole and Grice streets. Virtually everyone scrupulously avoided him. And then one day in 1932, Wilcox, with a shotgun in his hand, crept inside John Tuttle's garage on South Road Street. He sat down on a small stool in the corner, placed the end of the gun barrel against his head, and ended his own life.

Another chapter was written in the story about Jim Wilcox. To the younger generation, it was just another suicide; but to the older people in and around the Elizabeth City area, who had followed or attended the trial back in 1902, it was more.

It was the final chapter in the series of events that had led to the strange death of "Beautiful Nellie Cropsey." Now, after seventy years have passed, the murder is still an unsolved mystery. Today, while this book is being written, Mr. David Outlaw, eighty years old, and the last survivor of the main family tree of Mr. and Mrs. Edward Outlaw, Sr., lives alone in the Old Cropsey Mansion at 1109, Riverside Avenue, in Elizabeth City, North Carolina.

CHAPTER SIXTEEN

Conquerors and Tragedy

On July 10, 1901, Wilbur and Orville Wright once again left Dayton, Ohio, to return to the little hamlet at Kitty Hawk in North Carolina, where about a dozen widely scattered dwellings made up the tree-hidden village. Then to the south for a short distance, and down the beach to Kill Devil Hill, where high bleak sand hills stood waiting.

This time they planned to build a long shed out of boards instead of pitching a canvas tent. Also on the second exciting and dangerous undertaking, strong muslin cloth instead of sateen was to be used, because the close weave made it less porous.

Arriving three days later at Norfolk, Virginia, Orville and Wilbur made their way across the platforms and tracks at the Norfolk depot to the train that would take them to Elizabeth City. A few stops were made before crossing the state line into North Carolina.

Minutes later, the old Norfolk & Southern began slowing down, for the stop at Moyock, while her whistle screamed and tons of steel, making a screeching sound, came to a temporary halt on the tracks. Smoke circles closed in above the huge smokestack and slowly drifted off into space in the light breeze that blew from the south.

As Orville stepped from the train for a few moments, he was greatly impressed by the thundering sounds of hoofs as horses suddenly raced to a stop at the station hitching rail. Their riders leaped to the ground, leaving them prancing nervously and breathing hard, while clouds of dust rose in the air and marked their trail to the station.

Orville felt deafened by the piercing, prolonged sound of the whistle as he climbed aboard the train. Reeds and low-growing bushes alongside the tracks bowed and waved from the air pressure made by the train as it increased speed between the stops.

171

The next stop was Snowden, with about half a dozen houses, one little country store and post office, all conveniently built around the railroad station.

At this stop a mailman, who drove a very fast horse and buggy, met the train every day, picked up the mailbags, and headed south through Currituck County. After stopping at Sligo, Currituck, Maple, Barco, and Coinjock, he turned left about three miles south, off the main road, on the Upper Swamp Road that led to Aydlett one mile away. Then next to Poplar Branch, where the mailman traded horses, and continued across the Lower Swamp Road to Bertha, Grandy, Jarvisburg, Olds, Powels Point, Mamie, Spot, Harbinger, and Point Harbor, which was located at the extreme end of Currituck County, making this the last stop on his route for the day.

Rising early each morning, he repeated the same stops at these sixteen small post offices, dotted about the county, picking up the mail that was to be sent away, then back to Snowden at the Railroad Station for more mailbags because, rain or shine, snow or blow, the mail must go through.

The stop at Snowden took longer than elsewhere before reaching Elizabeth City, because at this point freight as well as mail going through Currituck County over the unpaved roads by horse-drawn carts, buggies, or wagons was unloaded here. While this was being done, Orville and Wilbur walked to the general store near the station. Wilbur, being rather distant, stopped to look at the long peppermint candy sticks on the counter. Orville, being more talkative, strolled on further and sat on a cracker barrel where the natives were busy chewing tobacco and swapping yarns. This is where Orville learned about the mail and freight routes through Currituck County.

Suddenly several short warning signals were heard; the whistle was calling all passengers aboard. The Old Iron Horse stood ready, belching black smoke from her stack. As the door closed behind the last passenger, the wheels began to turn and the train moved down the tracks toward the next stop at Shawboro.

During this age there were no stock laws. Hogs, sheep, horses, and cattle roamed about freely, grazing where they wished. Now and then an excited cow would dash in front of the train, striking violently against the fanlike iron grill that jutted out on the train only a few inches above the track. This grill would scoop

172

the cow up, carry her a few feet down the track, and usually dump her off to one side; thus rightfully it had earned the name of "cowcatcher" ever since the first Iron Horse had huffed and puffed her way across the desolate wilderness.

Shawboro was a very active little village, with a sawmill near the tracks, three general stores, a post office, and several dwellings in the area. After leaving Shawboro, and briefly stopping at Gregory Station, the train soon crossed the county line and over into Camden County where only two stops were made: one at Belcros and the other at Camden, four miles east of Elizabeth City.

The Wright Brothers arrived at the end of their journey by rail on schedule in Elizabeth City, at five-thirty in the afternoon. As they stepped from the train, Orville called Wilbur's attention to the low scuds of fleecy clouds that slowly moved across the sky. Long warm summer days were here. The sun began to lower in the west. Dark shadows lengthened down the street from tall spreading trees that lined the sidewalks, as they rode by horse and buggy toward the foot of Main Street and on to the Hotel Arlington.

At the Arlington a hot delicious home-cooked meal was enjoyed, and soon followed by a restful night's sleep, while the cool breezes from the Pasquotank River blew through the screen in the large open window across their beds. At the break of dawn, they were awakened by the continuous rumbling of thunder. Heavy rains poured down, and gusts of wind forced rain through the window screen before Wilbur could pull the window down. The thunder and rain soon passed, and Orville and Wilbur prepared to leave the hotel.

The rain-washed buildings and docks glistened and sparkled in the early morning sunlight. Mist that rose from the river disappeared as the sun soared to great heights. All morning, on July 14, 1901, the Wright brothers were busy. At the Kramer Brothers Lumber Company they purchased enough rough boards for the shed they planned to build at Kill Devil Hill. The boards were immediately loaded on wagons and delivered to the dock, where the *Hattie Creef*, patiently waited to carry the Wright brothers to Kitty Hawk. By 1:30 P.M., Captain Johnson finished checking his passenger list, all freight was on board, and the mail bag locked in its usual place in the pilothouse. Once more orders were given to shove off, and the sails were unfurled.

Orville and Wilbur sat on deck in canvas folding chairs, watching the low flat-top buildings gradually disappear out of sight on the horizon as the *Hattie Creef* sailed down the choppy amber waters of the Pasquotank River.

Gradually the wind ceased to some extent as they were crossing Albemarle Sound, and the *Hattie Creef* lost some of her power. This caused her to be late. But in spite of the wind behaving in this manner, at 5:30 they slowly sailed into Kitty Hawk Bay.

Captain Bill Tate, the man that had believed, helped, and encouraged Wilbur from the very beginning of the experiments, was waiting with a small flat-top barge.

Everyone helped. The lumber was quickly taken from the deck of the *Hattie Creef* and placed on the barge, along with the other boxes and crude-looking crates. Orville, Wilbur, and Captain Tate moved the barge toward shore, tugging and shoving until it struck bottom near the shore where it was anchored for the night.

Before daybreak, next morning, while the tide was low, Captain Tate backed his horse and cart down to the barge. Load after load was hauled ashore and left in a pile a few feet away from the waterline.

Two days later, by horse and cart, all the lumber had been moved over the hot sand to Kill Devil Hill. Wilbur and Orville continued to room and board at the Tates' while they worked long hours on their shed in the heat of the summer sun.

On August 30, 1901, the Wright brothers moved into their new home at Kill Devil Hill. The wood-frame shed was twenty-five feet long, sixteen feet wide, and seven feet high at the eaves. The shed faced south, away from the strong and cold winter winds. At the north end, on the east side, doors hinged near the top, when opened, provided an awning against the warm autumn sun. The south end of the shed was used for living quarters. One table, two-and-a-half by three-and-a-half feet, stood on the floor against the low wall. A quart-size gray enamel coffeepot, three straw-bottom chairs, and a washbowl and pitcher made up the largest part of the furniture. Food was prepared on a small oil stove, and an oil drum that lay on its side was used to burn driftwood for heat, when the weather was cold. Overhead, one on each side of the shed, were two bunks, made of canvas, drawn tight by ropes on all sides, and fastened to hollow metal pipes.

Here they assembled their second glider much larger and much different from the first one of 1900. Before returning this time, they had made more than two hundred and fifty types of wing surfaces at their Dayton, Ohio, workshop where they kept an accurate record of the tests that were made in a wind tunnel, all of which helped to bring about great progress in assembling their second experimental glider at Kitty Hawk.

This time they built the largest glider in the world. It weighed over six hundred pounds. The wingspan was four inches over forty feet. Each wing was six-and-a-half feet wide, and six-foot struts separated and held them together. A vertical rudder, with wires attached, was controlled from near the control center of the lower wing that was left uncovered. An eighteen-inch-wide space was provided for the operator. While lying belly down, the operator could control the wing-twister by moving his feet, to which were attached the control wires. By stretching his arms in front, he could control the rudder.

The glider was mounted on a pair of sled-like skids to protect the lower wings and rudder from scraping against the sand when taking off or landing.

Late in October, at Kill Devil Hill, the glider was again tested where the prevailing winds in this particular area blew just about right—a steady, strong, brisk breeze between twenty-five and thirty miles per hour. This test proved to be far more successful than the one Wilbur had made in the fall of 1900.

Early in the morning on December 15, taking their records with them after securing everything safely inside the shed from the danger of a storm and drifting sand, the Wright brothers waited in the cold bitter wind at the end of the wharf at Kitty Hawk for the *Hattie Creef*. After being aboard a few minutes, hot coffee, bacon, and eggs were served for breakfast. They had learned to depend on her for transportation between Kitty Hawk and Elizabeth City.

Four days later, Orville and Wilbur were safely back home in Dayton, Ohio, eager to bring their sister Katharine up to date with their test on their latest glider. At their bicycle shop, Wilbur continued to experiment with another glider. He made many

175

more changes. Orville helped, and also kept their business going to earn money for their experiments.

On September 17, 1902, the Wright brothers returned to Elizabeth City. When they arrived at the docks along the Pasquotank River, the *Hattie Creef* was waiting. Her huge canvas sails rustled vigorously in the strong west wind as the slack was taken up in the ropes, ready to set sail away from this busy little town to the rustic tree-hidden village at Kitty Hawk.

At Kill Devil Hill, early in October, sled-like runners four feet, eight inches apart, on a wooden monorail about sixty feet long with a thin band of metal fastened on top of the rail, were used for their takeoff strip. The monorail rigged so the glider would ride until it gathered enough speed to take off. This third machine also flew like a glider from the top of Kill Devil Hill, and proved very successful. Here Wilbur flew several feet controlling the glider with the wires by using his hands and feet. At this moment the air was in fact conquered by man. Now only an engine and a propeller were needed to keep the glider in the air and make it an airplane.

Returning home once more, they had no choice but to build their own engine. Charlie Taylor, their bicycle-shop mechanic, helped them make a 4-cylinder motor. It developed between 12 and 16 horsepower at 1,200 revolutions per minute. A tinsmith in Dayton made the gasoline tank about one foot long and three inches in diameter which held half a gallon of gasoline.

The engine was mounted on the lower wing of the glider, just to the right of center. Left of center, the Wright brothers designed an operator's seat or cradle with levers in easy reach of the wing warping wires. Then a pair of two-blade wooden propellers, making about 310 revolutions per minute, producing one hundred or more pounds of thrust were assembled.

Five days later, the *Hattie Creef* left the crowded docks at Elizabeth City and proudly sailed the same course, full speed ahead, having a strong fair wind in her sails, and gliding along over the dark waters in the Pasquotank River, with Wilbur and Orville on board. The engine and glider were crated in odd-looking boxes and placed where the brothers could keep a watchful eye on them, while returning to their shed at Kitty Hawk.

The hands of time moved on as the Wright brothers worked untiringly assembling their glider and gasoline engine, and getting ready for the real test. Then, on December 17, 1903, John T. Daniels, W. S. Dough, and A. D. Etheridge, all from the small Life Saving Station, along with W. C. Brinkley, a visiting lumber buyer from Manteo, and a sixteen-year-old boy Johnny Moore from Nags Head nearby, waited to help.

At 10:30 A.M. the engine was started. After coughing and wheezing several times it began a steady putt-putt. The bicycle chain began clanging along the sprocket or guides that pulled the propeller. Orville sat in the cradle, secured the wing-warping wires around his hips, and made sure that the front elevator controls were working.

Moments later, the glider slowly moved down the track on the wooden monorail. As it glided on the rail, it began to gather speed, six—seven—eight miles an hour. Suddenly it took off into the air. Mr. Daniels quickly clicked the camera. The picture was taken as Orville flew one hundred and twenty feet in twelve seconds, and landed smoothly without any mishap.

This was the first flight in the history of the world, in which a machine carrying a man had raised itself by its own power into the air and flew. The Wright brothers were visited by Octave Chanute of Chicago, and Dr. Sprat of Philadelphia. Both men were very interested in the brothers' success at Kill Devil Hill, and praised them for the progress they had made with their experiments.

At home the Wrights finished a still heavier plane on January 15, 1904, and flew it in a pasture eight miles from Dayton. But little progress was made during the next few months. Then, on September 20, 1904, they made their first complete circle. From then on, they really began to make progress in many ways.

Early on a Friday morning in October 1905, Wilbur flew for thirty-eight minutes, covering a circle on a course for twenty-four miles. Now people began to believe in miracles. During this period of history making, ladies' hats with extravagant arrangements of feathers, ribbons, and artificial fruits were often as awkward as their dresses. Truly the turn of the twentieth century was the beginning of many great changes, an age of miracles, the beginning of a decade of progress.

Faithfully, without any misfortune, the *Hattie Creef* made her runs between Manteo and Elizabeth City, under sail, through many storms and all kinds of weather. She became known as the most dependable means of transportation and communication between the Outer Banks and Elizabeth City, North Carolina. Many delicious meals were enjoyed on the way to and from the Outer Banks. Many young lovers sat on deck watching moonbeams spray the surface of the dark waters in the path of the bright moonlight ahead of the schooner. Many soft, cool, summer rains from low black clouds washed the decks as the hands of time moved on.

Then an unexpected tragedy struck the home of George Washington Creef., Jr. His lovely wife Ann became ill and died, leaving him with the three children, Ella, Hattie, and Hubert.

A few months later, when time began to heal the wounds, Wash married Ada Blivens Chappell, from Perquimins County. In due time Ada gave birth to two sons, Benjamin Allen and Paul Chappell Creef. Paul died at the age of four. (Ben Creef now lives at his residence at 306 Budleigh Street, with his attractive wife and children, in their beautiful brick home close to his father's old home in Manteo. Hubert A. Creef, Jr., also lives on the same Street, at 301 Budleigh, with his lovely wife, and children, in their two-story brick home.)

CHAPTER SEVENTEEN

Many Changes

In the fall, on October 18, 1907, George Washington Creef, Jr., had the *Hattie Creef* pulled out of the water and onto the railway, and left her to dry out for a few days. This was the same railway where this famous boat was built in 1889, along the shore of this historical island, at Manteo, North Carolina.

During the next few weeks, her sails and mast were removed. Also several other changes were taking place while two 10-horse Lathrope engines were installed. On March 3, 1908, after the changes had been completed, once again she slid down the railway and back into the cypress-stained waters of Shallowbag Bay.

For the following five months, Captain Martin Johnson and his crew continued to operate his ship as usual between these separated villages, carrying the customary cargo of freight, passengers, and mail, with some honeymoon couples in the group.

Wind, or no wind, now with her 10-horse Lathrope engines, the *Hattie Creef* ran her route on schedule—leaving Manteo at six o'clock in the morning, and returning at six o'clock in the evening, with no trouble at all plowing through the dark ruffled waters of the Albemarle Sound and the Pasquotank River.

Many people from Edenton, Hertford, and Elizabeth City enjoyed several cruises on the *Hattie Creef*, where scenic moss-draped cypress trees jutted out at many points along the shore, sparkling in the sunlight. Some from Camden and Currituck counties made trips to the beach on their vacations, with several people stopping off at Hollowell's Pier on the sound side at Nags Head, where they could walk about a mile across the windblown sand ripples, through the low-scattered hanging bushes and beach grass, to the surf.

At the foot of the pier, a few feet away from the shore end, stood a long two-story wooden building. On the first floor, a post office occupied a very small space. The rest of the floor was used for general merchandise, and had the makings of an old general store to meet the needs of the natives as well as the summer vacationers.

The top-floor space was divided into several small unfinished rooms to provide sleeping accommodations for tourists and vacationers. The building was owned by Graham Hollowell, a native of Elizabeth City, and known as the Hollowell Hotel. About half-a-mile to the north stood the highest sand hills along the Atlantic coastline, known as Jockey Ridge. Now thousands of people the year round, especially during the summer months, climb to the top of this huge mass of shifting sand for a wonderful view of the broad blue Atlantic Ocean, and watch the ships as they travel the sea-lanes and have an excellent view of the surrounding Outer Banks including historical Roanoke Island.

At that time there were very few houses on the beach. Only scattered roughly built shacks stood miles apart, with a few on the sound side at Nags Head where typical sand dunes resembled great ocean waves covered with small ripples and large masses of windblown dry sand exposed to the mercy of nature took on many curious attractive shapes. Here the dunes were constantly changing and shifting, except in scattered places where trees, plants, sea oats, and patches of grass managed to overrun and capture them.

On August 5, 1908, Captain Martin Johnson turned the historic *Hattie Creef* over to Captain Llewellyn Cudworth. Dan Davis was engineer, and Fred Creef the cook. For the next three years daily trips were made from Manteo, stopping to Hollowells Pier at Nags Head, Kitty Hawk, Newberns' Landing, Jarvisburg, and Grandy, then on to Elizabeth City. The vessel continuously gave superior service and pleasure, as usual, to all, as well as rescue to those in need or in times of trouble.

Today the southwest wind blew strong, whipping up choppy waves that splashed against the sides of the *Hattie Creef*, making gurgling noises as she left Albemarle Sound and entered the Pasquotank River, where low-scattered and thinly ferned pale-green cypress trees outlined the shore on each side of the river, especially after passing Hospital Point, as it narrowed coming into the harbor.

Scraggy moss-covered piling rose a few inches above the water along the shoreline and near the shackly wooden bridge, the only link that connected Elizabeth City with Camden County, and the only bridge that spanned the river at this narrow point. On the left along the waterfront, at the end of a familiar two-story brick building, the name Hotel Arlington was displayed in large white letters. Next was N. G. Grandy, Wholesale Grocery. On the other side of the bridge, The Crystal Ice and Coal Company, established by William Edward Dunston in 1894, proudly displayed its sign beside that of W. J. Woodley, who had opened for business in 1890 as a wholesale grocery. Later, between these two well-known business firms, came the Globe Fish Company, Inc., established by E. R. and A. S. Daniels in 1911. Both were natives of Wancheese, on Roanoke Island.

On April 25, 1910, the historical ship was rebuilt. It now had a long high stateroom for passengers, large enough to serve meals easily to all on board. This time she was put on what was known as the Currituck run for the next two years, transporting farm produce and passengers to Elizabeth City.

In 1912 she was sold by the Creef's to the Eastern Carolina Transportation Company, to transport boxes of fish and other cargo, calling on the ports of Manns Harbor, Stumpy Point, Rodanthia, and Wancheese, and continuing on to Elizabeth City. At the docks of the Globe Fish Company, Inc., the fish were unloaded, and some were sold locally; but the bulk was repacked to be shipped to many faraway markets all over the country.

On September 14, 1914, S. M. Daniels of Wancheese, North Carolina, sold the *Hattie Creef*, to the Globe Fish Company, Inc. The new owners used her exclusively to transport fish from Dare County fish houses to Elizabeth City for the Globe Fish Company, Inc. After several months of service, she was again hauled out of the water on the railway, and her motors were changed, this time installing a 3-cylinder, 45-horsepower, Fairbanks-Morse engine.

Ezekiel Daniels, one of the owners of the Globe Fish Company, originally came from the famous fishing village at Wancheese, located at the south end of Roanoke Island, where the waters of the spacious Pamlico Sound continue to bathe its shores, and where a variety of the finest fish in the world are caught by expert fishermen.

Zeke Daniels, as he was better known by the people along the Outer Banks and in Elizabeth City, was a large fish merchant for many years. He bought practically all the fish caught along the Outer Banks, using the *Hattie Creef* to transport the boxes of fish to the Globe Fish Company at Elizabeth City. He also operated an old general store. Zeke Daniels was very prosperous, and grew in wealth as the hands of time slowly but surely left the present moments and events behind and moved into an unknown future.

Many people had worked on the *Hattie Creef* at different times, including Banister Davis and Crawford Daniels, both of Wancheese. Truxton Midgett, a retired Lieutenant Commander of the United States Coast Guard (now living at his native home in Kitty Hawk), made several runs on this eminent vessel.

During certain times of the year shad came in from the Atlantic Ocean through Oregon Inlet and into Pamlico Sound, which is about twenty miles wide. Roe shad were plentiful. They were sold on the markets all over the country, and brought a very high price. While the shad were plentiful, the faithful untiring *Hattie Creef* ran night and day on her regular runs, loaded with boxes of these valuable fish.

It was late in the afternoon. Streaks of golden misty shafts of sunlight from the setting sun, through open spaces in the dark-green forest along the tall steep banks near the north end of Roanoke Island, crossed her path and brought pleasing memories of the past, haunting her while the *Hattie Creef* moved under a shelter of gloom. This island seemed an enchanted whirl of magnificent veils of silent sunlight, with ghosts of white and gray lazy shadows slowly moving as the sun hung just above the uneven groves of beautiful wild trees, so real yet seemingly a dream, while leaving this mystifying island behind and beginning her journey across the Albermarle Sound.

On September 1, 1916, Ed Pugh of Elizabeth City, shipped with the Globe Fish Company, Inc., on the *Hattie Creef*, as engineer, replacing Dan Davis, Captain Llewellyn Cudworth stayed at the wheel, and Fred Creef still continued to be the cook.

During the next twelve months many tons of fish were moved from the fish houses along the Outer Banks region, along with a few passengers, to the Globe Fish Company.

The winter of 1917 will long be remembered by many older people as the Winter of the Big Freeze. In January, late in the afternoon, while the *Hattie Creef* was moored alongside the wharf at the fish house in Wancheese, the sky suddenly began to darken.

The wind roared out of the north, and whitecaps were formed on the waves in Pamlico Sound as sunset, twilight, and night fell upon the island.

By midnight, temperatures had dropped to five degrees above zero. Snowflakes fell and began to wrap the island's wonders. At dawn the wind shifted around to the northeast and began to lull, while the temperature fell to ten degrees below zero. For the next few days the sky was dark and heavy overcast hovered near, and the mercury remained below zero.

All the sounds, rivers, and lakes were frozen; some of the ice in North and Pasquotank rivers was from four to five feet thick. Several people from Currituck and Camden counties walked across the ice to Elizabeth City, and one young man crabbed along driving his Model-T car.

Three weeks later, the mercury rose to normal, the ice began to melt and lose its strength, and the *Hattie Creef* awoke and left her berth.

On May 11, 1920, Ed Pugh retired as engineer. Captain Cudworth also decided to ship with another company. No time was lost during the changeover. Edward Davis of Wancheese immediately took the job as engineer, and Captain Casper D. Meekins was hired by the Globe Fish Company, Inc. These two men were experienced navigators in all kinds of weather in these sounds and rivers, where tons of fish must constantly be kept moving to Elizabeth City. This was truly a thriving business. The Daniels, owners of the Globe, were very prosperous and grew in wealth.

For the next nineteen years, Edward Davis and Casper Meekins remained with the *Hattie Creef* and made many, many successful runs through storms, wild winds, rough waters, sleet and hail; through calm waters of the Albemarle Sound and the peaceful Pasquotank River, at times where laughter, loneliness, sudden cool summer rain showers fell, and where full moons and starlit nights passed the lonely hours with the hands of time without a whine or whimper.

On and on she plowed her way through the brownish-yellow waters, across the sounds and rivers, to and from the land of mystery along the Outer Banks where widely scattered villages and fishing hamlets lay in a world of their own.

Up near the north end of Roanoke Island, where the finest of all grapes grow on the large Scuppernong grapevine close to the shores of Roanoke Sound, the scenic views are magnificent where Mother Vineyard, supposedly the original of all scuppernong vines over three hundred years old, still remains one of the historical wonders of North Carolina. Was it here, or had it been transplanted to Roanoke Island from England by members of the Lost Colony? No one really has the answer. Here is where the famous, well known yaupon bushes grow wild. The leaves and twigs are picked, dried, and used to make tea, a favorite mealtime drink with the natives along the Outer Banks for many centuries. During the winter months the yaupon bushes produce bright-red berries, so numerous they are often used for Christmas holiday decorations.

During the years that the *Hattie Creef* was making history many unforgettable important events had also taken place, such as World War I, which began in 1914 and ended in 1918. Woodrow Wilson was President of the United States for eight years during that struggle North Carolina sent 86,000 men into the Armed Forces.

Then came the Great Depression, which began in 1929, while Herbert Hoover was President. Farmers suffered more than other classes; many of them lost their farms and homes. Cotton dropped to five cents a pound from the wartime price of forty cents. Wages and salaries were cut again and again. More people were thrown out of work. Banks all over the country failed.

But the *Hattie Creef* kept up the good work of transporting load after load of the best fish in the world, and the Globe Fish Company Inc., continued to enjoy prosperity in spite of all the difficulties the country was experiencing. Then, in 1933, Franklin D. Roosevelt became President of the United States. He realized the critical condition the country was in and called Congress to special session. This was the beginning of the New Deal, and soon the country began to once more stand on its own feet.

Meanwhile, during the intervening events, as the hands of time moved on, out into the unknown, George Washington Creef, Jr., became ill and died on February 10, 1928, at the age of seventy-two. He was laid to rest in the cemetery at Manteo, on Roanoke Island, North Carolina.

In the spring of 1928, during the squeeze of the Great Depression, with the growing world on wheels, the need for a link across Currituck Sound between Point Harbor and the beach near Kitty Hawk was discussed by some of the leading citizens in the Albemarle area. Soon it was decided that a toll bridge would be the answer. Work immediately began, with L. C. Blades, as president and W. G. Gaither, Sr., as Secretary and Treasurer. After nearly two years of hard labor over the water in the hot summer sun and shrinking from the piercing cold winter winds while removing many stumblingblocks, the wooden bridge was completed. It was two and three-fourths miles long.

This toll bridge was opened for business on September 27, 1930. It was a very important step, linking the Outer Banks with the mainland. Now cars, trucks, and buses rolled on to their destinations. The price of these bleak, sandy beach lots began to soar, where not so long ago this worthless sand sold from fifty-cents to one dollar per acre.

CHAPTER EIGHTEEN

Unprepared

On January 16, 1939, the Globe Fish Company sold the *Hattie Creef* to J. J. Wilkinson of Elizabeth City. Captain Casper Meekins and his engineer, Edward Davis of Wancheese, quit their jobs on the faithful ship and returned to their homes after nineteen years of service.

Captain Jess Wilkinson owned a few river barges and a small tugboat. After removing the passenger cabin and making other necessary changes at the Elizabeth City Shipyard, on Riverside Avenue, a 45-horsepower Diesel motor was installed in order that she could be used as a tugboat.

Later again, the *Hattie Creef* proved herself worthy and outstanding, but the strain from pulling heavy barges loaded with sand, sometimes pebbles, or logs caused considerable vibration. After a few years of this strenuous heavy duty she began to quiver and tremble, causing her seams to gradually loosen, and creating slow leaks in several places. Soon she was back on the cradle at the Elizabeth City Shipyard, where her seams were calked, her bottom painted, and then she was back in service and chugging through the dark waters of the rivers, sounds, and lakes.

Meanwhile, on December 7, 1941, the United States was plunged into the World War II in a surprise attack by the Japanese on our chief naval base at Pearl Harbor, in the Hawaiian Islands in the Pacific Ocean. The attack came early on Sunday morning, destroying several warships, many airplanes, and killing about 4,700 of our men. Within a few days the United States was at war with Japan, Italy, and Germany.

Striking without warning at dawn, on September 1, 1939, the German Air Force caught the Polish Air Force on its various airfields and destroyed it. The mechanized might of Germany crushed Poland in a matter of days. The Western World was unprepared; the German *Luftwaffe* controlled the air.

While the Western Powers were desperately trying to recover

from a great crippling and embarrassing depression, the German war plants were running night and day in preparation for another world war. While other countries cut back on their military strength, and moth-balled their fleets, Germany was arming to the teeth under the powerful leadership of Adolf Hitler.

At the outbreak of World War II, the democratic world, already disillusioned and paralyzed, wondered about the outcome of Western Civilization. Nazi Germany boasted that their air force was capable of destroying all the cities in the world. And for the next two years these threats appeared to be justified as the countries in Europe fell, one after another, before the invincible military machine as it swept on to victory after victory.

On June 25, 1940, after only five days of fighting, the collapse of France was the worst sudden military disaster in history. Hitler's mighty armies rolled on to the English Channel, only twenty-four miles away from Great Britain, where the Nazis suddenly shifted to massive daylight bombing attacks on London, the world's largest city.

The destruction and suffering were immense. Remember the German Empire under Bismarck and Kaiser Wilhelm II? How the Kaiser dismissed Bismarck two years after he became Emperor, and gained complete control over his country? Under the Kaiser's rule, Germany's spectacular achievements excited the fear and wonder as well as the admiration of the rest of the world. His military power was the German Empire, whose armies came close to conquering all of Europe in World War I.

Now, under an equally capable intelligent dictator, Germany had risen again to be the most powerful nation on earth. Many readers will remember, back in 1918, when the British Navy was as supreme on the high seas as the German Army on land. Britain's sea power enabled her to control an empire that included one-fourth of all the territory and people of the world. What has happened to Great Britain's leadership? Today, with only a skeleton Navy, she has lost control of the seas and a large part of her territory, while other nations take the lead.

The purpose of this brief history about the events that took place during the time when the *Hattie Creef* was still very active, is only to refresh or revive the memory of those who read this book.

Hitler's mighty army rolled on and on, crushing everything in its path. But suddenly the picture changed, in May and June of 1940, after the French Army and the Maginot Line ceased to exist. The British Navy was in serious danger. German submarines roamed the oceans furtively in search of their prey.

In March 1941, President Roosevelt urged Congress to pass the Lend Lease Act. Soon an American ship was sunk in the South Atlantic. Again, in October 1941, two American destroyers, while on convoy duty near Iceland, were torpeoded by German submarines and many lives were lost. The shooting war had really started.

On December 7, 1941, early Sunday morning, a large squadron of carrier-based Japanese bombers and torpedo planes sneaked into Pearl Harbor and crippled or sank eight battleships, three destroyers, and a number of cruisers. The next day, December 8, the United States Congress declared war on Japan. Three days later, Italy, Germany, and Japan declared war on the United States.

America's industrial potential and resources were enormous, but how long would it take to mobilize them? The war now raged in Russia, the Mediterranean Sea, Western Europe, and in the Pacific.

At this point, the United States, Great Britain, and Russia joined hands to crush this mighty onslaught. In December 1941, the extremely cold winter helped to stop the Germans in Russia. They lacked proper clothing, and many froze to death.

Then, in June 1942, the Germans again marched on Russia. This time they reached Stalingrad. But after six months in January 1943, after the Russians closed in behind the Germans and captured almost 300,000 of them.

The crucial battle on the Mediterranean and the Western European Front was fought on Egyptian soil by Montgomery's superior Eighth Army.

After crippling our fleet at Pearl Harbor, the Japanese were on the move in the pacific Ocean, capturing American islands—Guam, the Philippines, and Wake. Also Malaya, British Hong Kong, and the Dutch East Indies were overrun by the Japs.

In May 1942, a reinforced American Fleet turned back a strong Japanese Fleet in the battle of the Coral Sea, near Australia. Again the American Fleet clashed with the Japanese and fought at long range in the battle off Midway Island, entirely from carriers by aircraft and submarines, and sank all four of the Japanese carriers before the Japanese commander ordered his ships to withdraw.

Early in November 1942, under the command of General Dwight D. Eisenhower, troops were landed in French North Africa, and by February 1943, with the help of Montgomery's troops, forced Rommel to surrender. After conquering the Island of Sicily in the Mediterranean Sea, the American Forces invaded the southern part of Italy. Mussolini, Italy's ruler, was soon overthrown by his own military leaders.

By 1944 the Allies had gained mastery of the skies, and on June 6, 1944, troops were successfully landed on the Normandy Coast under heavy fire from the Germans. Early in 1945, American and British Forces joined the French units and broke through the German lines, or West Wall. Then they crossed the Rhine River and joined up with Russian units along the banks of Elbe River. After a die-hard stand, Germany surrendered on May 8, 1945.

Meanwhile American Forces under General Douglas Mac-Arthur, with a powerful naval escort, began to take island after island in the Pacific. The American Fleet under the command of Admiral Chester Nimitz, definitely superior to the Japanese Fleet, steamed westward toward Japan and captured Japanese-held territory everywhere.

In October 1944, landings in the Philippines brought the Japanese Fleet out for a last desperate try to stave off the powerful and eager American Fleet. This brought on the greatest naval battle in history—the battle of Leyte Gulf, where the Japanese Fleet was entirely destroyed.

Rather than uselessly sacrifice any more lives, which a direct landing on the Japanese home islands would cause, it was decided to use the atomic bomb to horrify Japan into surrender. The first atomic bomb ever to be used in warfare was dropped on the Japanese city of Hiroshima, destroying it on August 6, 1945. On August 9, the second atomic bomb was dropped on another Japanese city, demolishing the industrial city of Nagasaki. Five days later, on August 14, 1945, Japan surrendered. World War II was ended.

Over twenty-two million people had been killed, and over thirty-four million wounded, not to mention the property damage and broken homes left behind. President Roosevelt died on April 12, 1945, before the war ended, only a few months before the defeat of Germany and Japan.

In the meantime the loyalty of the *Hattie Creef* was left unquestioned, because during the course of grinding out the uncertainty of the great problems that faced the world in those changing years she continued to churn the amber-colored waters of the sounds and rivers, both day and night, wherever she was needed.

Again she was temporarily secured at the dock beside the big cradle at the Elizabeth City Shipyard, while the blocking was being shifted around on the cradle to fit under her bottom. Soon the engine was started in the pumphouse by Captain Adrew Sanders. The brake that held the large winch was released, and the long cradle slowly began to disappear beneath the *Hattie Creef*, in the dark restless waters of the Pasquotank River. Moments later the cable around the winch began to get taut as the cradle cautiously crawled out of the water, leaving the boat resting on the blocks, while Captain Ernest J. Sanders, one of the owners of the shipyard, watched from his office window nearby.

Two weeks later, after her seams were calked and her bottom painted, she was ready to return to her master for service.

For the next three and a half years she was used continuously until September 25, 1949. After then Captain Jess Wilkinson's business became less active, and his boats were very old. The *Hattie Creef* was slowly taking in water through the stuffing box as well as in some of her seams around her stern on the starboard side. Captain Wilkinson's health was beginning to decline, and he knew that he must retire.

On the Camden side of the Pasquotank River, a suitable resting place was found near the shore at a small wooden wharf alongside the huge stone bridge that spans the river at this narrow point. Here the historical *Hattie Creef* was safely moored, now free from many of the dangers she had encountered during the years over a long period of time.

At her resting place, the wind whined in the scattered pines and in the low-ferned cypress trees that formed the shoreline near her bow, where green moss-covered piling rose just above the surface of the reddish-brown cypress water and provided places where birds and gulls could rest or sleep.

An automatic bilge pump was properly installed. The cabin doors were closed and locked, and the hatches secured before leaving her indefinitely. Sometimes she was rocked day and night in the wake on the water caused by a passing boat and lulled to sleep at night by gentle sounds as the wind moaned steadily through the trees. She was moored here to be forgotten, after pioneering and paving a road for better living by better transportation and communication for sixty years for the people along the Outer Banks of historical North Carolina.

For the next four years, little or no attention was given to this worthy outstanding boat. Ivy vines found shelter among the clusters of evergreen water bushes that grew along the shore, overhanging the water's edge near her bow and reaching out in an effort to touch her prow. Large brown marsh rabbits soon became accustomed to her presence, and paid her regular visits at twilight. Here they played and ate tender grass buds in the gloom, where the shore end of the sleepy little wharf stood in silence. Limbs and branches in the pale-green cypress trees nearby provided a roost for birds and crows to rest and sleep for the night.

Darkness covered the area: loneliness filled the cool night air. Against the clear glass windows in the pilothouse shone a faint gleam of starlight.

On June 10, 1943, the automatic bilge pump failed to operate after midnight. Water began building up in the bilges, and slowly the *Hattie Creef* began to sink at her stern beneath the peaceful dark waters of the Pasquotank River.

At daybreak the bridge-tender was the first to find her sunk, and news traveled swiftly over the area in Elizabeth City. Was this the end, or would she rise again?

CHAPTER NINETEEN

Alone

Claude Lewark, a native of Currituck County but now living on Pennsylvania Avenue in Elizabeth City, rushed to the aid of the *Hattie Creef*. The stern was submerged beneath the water, but her forward deck and pilothouse were still above the surface of the water and resting on the bottom.

After learning that the agreement between the Globe Fish Company, Inc., and J. J. Wilkinson had not been fulfilled, Captain Lewark immediately began making arrangements to buy the boat for himself. While growing up in Currituck County he had learned a few facts about the history of the *Hattie Creef*, before and after the turn of the century, and he became very much influenced by her past.

On June 15, 1953, R. E. Daniels, president of the Globe Fish Company, Inc., sold the *Hattie Creef* to Claude Lewark and his wife, Margarett Ann Blades Lewark, of 907 Pennsylvania Avenue, Elizabeth City, Pasquotank County, North Carolina.

The present owners of the Globe Fish Company, Inc., are R. P. Daniels, president, and R. E. Daniels, secretary and treasurer, descendants of the well-known Daniels Clan of Wancheese, on Roanoke Island in North Carolina. The Daniels are a great asset to the community in Elizabeth City, and are very prosperous.

Immediately after the purchase, Captain Lewark nailed sheets of plywood around the hatch on the aft end so that the top edge of the plywood would be a few inches above the surface of the water. Then he used a small barge, equipped with a pumping engine and large suction hose. The three-inch hose was dropped into the bilge through the hatch. Moments later, a large powerful stream of water was passing through the pump, forced on through another hose, and back into the river.

After four hours of pumping, the stern slowly began to rise

192

to the surface, and soon the *Hattie Creef* was leisurely swaying back and forth, using the slack in her hawser, swinging with ease in the light breeze and slow-moving tide. Without delay, the bilge pumps were repaired and put back into operation. Three days later she was towed about half a mile to the Elizabeth City Shipyard for some changes. She remained on the cradle until the necessary repairs were completed.

Before leaving the shipyard, a 150-horsepower, diesel electric engine was installed which worked like a charm—as if it had magical power. A few trial runs were made before she was tied up at the Basnight Boat Works, which consisted of a boathouse and a narrow dock directly across the river from where she had been moored when she sank. Now she was on the Elizabeth City side of the river, with her bow a few feet away from Water Street.

Throughout the entire summer and fall months Captain Lewark, with his family and friends, made many enjoyable pleasure trips cruising down the Pasquotank River, leaving the sleepy little harbor behind; turning left around Camden Point, soon crossing North River, and entering the mouth of Coinjock Canal; enjoying every moment watching the beautiful wild hollyhocks, waterlillies, and dogwood trees along the banks.

South winds blew gently across the water, cooling the air and causing them to pay less attention to the heat from the blazing summer sun. Many people came near while the *Hattie Creef* was tied up for a few minutes near Coinjock Bridge before traveling on by water to Great Bridge, Virginia, where the Lewarks were to visit friends. The presence of this historical boat as she entered every port was felt. It was amusing to watch the expressions on the faces of curious onlookers.

During the fall months, especially late in October, Captain Lewark and family traveled north for about thirty miles through the famous Dismal Swamp Canal that had been dug during George Washington's Administration. This canal was dug with slave labor, through a large tract of land which consisted of 150,000 acres. The canal begins a little south of Norfolk, Virginia, and extends into North Carolina. This tract was formerly covered with trees, with almost impervious brushwood between them; but now parts of it have been cleared and drained. In the middle of the swamp is a lake called Lake Drummond's Pond,

193

seven miles long. This dismal swamp, navigable canal extends north and south for about thirty miles, connecting Chesapeake Bay in Virginia, near Norfolk, with the Albemarle Sound, by way of the Pasquotank River.

In the month of October, sailing through this canal, the natural scenery is unbelievable. Wildflowers of many brilliant colors outline its vine-covered, tall banks. Overhanging various trees, with richly colored gold, purple, red, and orange autumn leaves, framed the renowned *Hattie Creef* on each side as she moved through the dark-colored cypress water in the narrow canal. In some places the full sun shone down; other places were partially shaded.

Then, in April 1958, she was moored beside the dock at Basnight Boat Works, and fully equipped for commercial crabbing in the Pasquotank River and Albemarle Sound. Many tons of crabs were taken from the rivers and sounds to the canning factory where they were processed for shipment all over the world.

In July 1961, the old motor was replaced with a 6-cylinder Mack-Diesel Electric, 440 volts. With power to spare, the *Hattie Creef* was now used by Captain Lewark to tow his dredge over several miles of water wherever the dredging work was to be done. Working from Perquimins River to Winton and Plymouth and many other places on the Chowan River, before returning to Elizabeth City.

The dredge was sold to a construction company in 1965. Soon the *Hattie Creef* was made fast to the dock, resting at her berth and floating in the water like a proud old duck sitting on a nest. After paving many thousand miles of progress in transportation and communication for the betterment of mankind, a sign tacked to the side of her pilothouse read: "For Sale."

Passersby stopped to stare; and out of state cars, catching a glimpse as they slowly rolled down the bridge that spaned the river, parked their cars on Water Street and walked back for a closer look. It was late in the afternoon as her owner stood on deck beside the pilothouse, answering questions asked by passing strangers. Her bow was only a few feet away from the Street facing West, in the path where the low-setting sun hung just above the rooftops and blazed a brilliant trail across her bow.

Intense emotional excitement mounted as this historical boat

194

attracted attention. Heads turned her way to catch a quick glimpse on their way to work. Magnificent columns of sunlight, the color and luster of gold, shone through the great stone bridge from the rosy flush of sunrise and shot forth across the *Hattie Creef* as she lay shrouded in the early morning mist, feeding the masses of hungry eyes that gazed upon her.

In September 1967, Captain Lewark sold the vessel to Elijah W. Tate of Coinjock, Currituck County, North Carolina. (He is the son of the late Captain Bill Tate, who was so helpful to the Wright brothers throughout their experiments at Kitty Hawk on the high Kill Devil Hill sand dunes.) Early in the day on September 5, her motor was started, her hawsers were untied from the piling at the dock and coiled on deck near the bow and stern. The whistle blew a loud, clear, shrilling sound that was so familiar to the bridge-tender. While the draw was raised, the *Hattie Creef* slowly passed through the opening and sailed on the amber-colored water of the Pasquotank River for the last time.

After seventy-eight years of service, leaving behind many un-forgettable memories of the past, she traveled on where every road led closer to home. Suddenly swinging around Camden Point, and after crossing North River, she entered Coinjock Canal. For the next few days she was made fast to the piling alongside the high canal bank in front of Captain Elijah Tate's home.

To him she provided quiet enjoyment, as he stood on his front porch with only a narrow pebbled road between his home and the canal bank where she was moored, because he was so closely acquainted with her past.

Later, numerous enjoyable cruising runs were made, along with his son Bill and his lovely wife Elizabeth, in Currituck Sound during the warm autumn days in September and October. Late in November near nightfall, during a rosy sunset just before twilight, along the canal bank in the forest, the wild shapes of tall trees silhouetted against the sky lingered a moment longer then disappeared into a cloud of darkness.

Suddenly the wind roaded out of the north, stripping a nearby maple and oak tree of their coat of autumn leaves, mixed with large scattered drops of rain that made strange noises against the windows. Almost all night strong gusts of wind, making a mournful sound, drove heavy rain showers against the house.

Just before dawn the wind moved around to the northwest, clearing the sky, and stars sparkled like diamonds.

Moments later, day broke clear but cold, and temperatures dropped below freezing. Captain Elijah Tate immediately secured the *Hattie Creef* at her mooring for the long winter months ahead.

On March 5, 1968, after a cold and stormy winter, Captain Elijah pulled the boat out of the water, up on his own railway, where the motor was removed and replaced her old original 1910-model engine with a 3-cylinder, 36-horsepower Palmer engine.

Early in April she was put back into the canal, her engine was started, a sudden signal was sounded on her whistle, and the bridge slowly began to open. Little did the *Hattie Creef* know that this was the last time her loud and clear whistle would signal a bridge-tender for permission to pass through the draw.

By noon, after leaving the canal at the west end, she entered North River and headed south. Black, unkept rough piling, partially outlined the shape of the old Barnetts Creek Wharf opposite the farming village at Grandy; there farmers once depended on river boats to load and transport their farm produce to the wharfs at Elizabeth City, where they were reloaded into boxcars that stood waiting on the tracks near the sheds by the river then shipped to faraway markets. Many thousand wooden barrels, full of Irish and sweet potatoes, were loaded at these wharfs.

Back in the horse and buggy days, when the Village Blacksmith was kept busy shaping and repairing the needs of the villagers with his forge, tongs, anvil, and hammer, he was the man who inspired the famous American poet, Henry Wadsworth Longfellow, to write "The Village Blacksmith."

Gone are the days when barrel factories were conveniently located in every farming community. Gone were the days when children and young "lovers" strolled the countryside in spring, searching for wild columbine, spring beauty, and wild blue phlox in the fields during the summer months; where evening primrose, wild strawberries grew, and green-bordered fields were filled with scarlet poppies rippling in a gentle summer breeze. Gone the sweet smell of the wild honeysuckle that filled the warm air. No more strolls in the autumn fields, where the English gentian, black-eyed Susan, yellow daisies and goldenrods once grew in abundance among the pink lady's-slippers and nodding lilies.

196

The sudden harsh, shrilling cry of a fish hawk as he darted across the bow of the *Hattie Creef* quickly brought Captain Elijah back from the past. Others quietly sat on scraggy projecting piling near the shore as they passed the abandoned Jarvisburg Pier that now was only a skeleton and merely a memory.

Gulls followed the *Hattie Creef* unnoticed, as she cut her way through the dark-brown cypress water in North River, passing a neighboring boat now and then, before she entered Albemarle Sound. The sun was slowly sinking in the west; the wind blew a steady cool breeze from the east, whipping up a sea of low rolling waves.

Captain Tate leisurely swung his boat to the left, around Point Harbor, and soon entered Currituck Sound, where the great stone bridge, named in honor of the Wright brothers appeared and began to take shape off the port bow in the distance only a few minutes away. The Wright Brothers Memorial Bridge spans Currituck Sound from Point Harbor, for a distance of two and three-fourths miles, to the beach near Kitty Hawk, with a high rise over the deep channel midway in the sound.

Now running parallel with the bridge, churning the water, completing her last mile in the sound, the boat proudly held her head high as cars, trucks, and buses roared over the magnificent bridge, making it seem more like a dream. At the beach end of the bridge, near Fisherman's Wharf, she anchored for the night.

In the early hours of the morning, wild ducks flew swiftly over the surface of the water. The cool keen air, the fresh smell of salty mist from the broad Atlantic, the bright color of wildflowers along the shore, told that the time was early spring. Crows cawed from their nests in the tall pine trees along the bush-lined banks.

Heavy moving equipment roared down the modern highway, turning off at the foot of the Wright Brothers Memorial bridge, stopping at the edge of the water, only a few feet away from the famous boat. John Ferebee, one of the ablest house-moving men in the country, was ready for business. A strong steel cable using two blocks and falls, was fastened around the boat and hooked to a large spreading pine tree. With the help of a wrecking truck, along with heavy duty machinery, the *Hattie Creef* was skidded up on the shore and out of the water.

Shovels were used for digging holes under her keel. Powerful

Jacks placed in the holes under her keel soon raised her high enough so that blocks could be placed under her bottom, along the sides. Gradually the boat was raised until the carrier could be placed in the right position and made fast to her bottom. Huge wheels on the World War II Army truck, equipped with four-wheel drive, began to move slowly ahead with ease, up the sloping low bank, through scattered underbrush, finally stopping on the highway about one thousand feet from the shoreline. Here a Highway Patrolman waited to escort the *Hattie Creef*, down the Highway on U.S. Bypass No. 158, for a distance of four-and-a-half miles. Forty-five minutes later, she was placed on blocks at her final resting place, on the south side of the Kitty Hawk Road, at the intersection of U.S. No. 158 Bypass.

She now sits alone on a parcel of lonely windblown sandy land, among the Kitty Hawk sand dunes. Where the wind forms a sea of ripples on the surface of the sand and sea oats play and toss their heads in the ocean breeze that sweeps across the beach.

After seventy-nine years of service, she rests alone, three and one-half miles north of the Wright Brothers National Memorial Monument watching the powerful, sweeping candle-light beams encircling the monument at Kill Devil Hill on her starboard side; alone where she can dream, collecting stardust that is washed away by the same rains, the same snowflakes and winds that have swept across the bleak sand dunes along the coast of the Outer Banks of historical North Carolina since the beginning of time, while the hands of time reach out into the unknown. Truly a living, historical monumental museum.

Gateway

Fruit Tree Overhanging Settler's Log Cabin

Transformed by "The Hands of Time"
A tree that stood along the shore of Roanoke Island.

A Deer on Roanoke Island
Game was plentiful in the early times.

Here the Wright Brothers Lived While Inventing the Plane.

7 Hawthorne Street, about 1900. Here the Wrights lived while inventing the plane.

Marker at Tate Home

The Wrights' First Glider, Kitty Hawk, 1900

Addie Tate's Sewing Machine
It was on this machine that the cloth for the glider wings was sewn.
(Now in Hattie Creef Museum)

Captain Bill Tate
He was a staunch friend of the Wrights at Kitty Hawk.

Wilbur Wright in Glider, 1902

Kitty Hawk Camp and Plane, 1911

Wilbur Wright on deck of the "Hattie Creef," 1911

Life Saving Station, Kill Devil Hills

Wright Brothers Memorial, Kill Devil Hills

Living Quarters of the Kill Devil Hills Hangar, 1903

James Wilcox and Ella Maud Cropsey from contemporary
sketches published in The Economist, a predecessor to The
Daily & Sunday Advance.

Jim Wilcox and Nellie Cropsey

The Cropsey Home On Riverside Avenue
Nellie Cropsey's mother watched the river, patiently, and with uncertainty, from the tower room.

Old Red Brick Jail at Elizabeth City
This is where Jim Wilcox was held. It is still in use.

Sign at Pasquotank County Courthouse

urthouse Where Jim Wilcox Was Tried.

The "Hattie Creef," High and Dry at Kitty Hawk

Fish in the Surf Or from the Pier, Dare County, N. C.

Cypress Trees on Pasquotank River, Near Cropsey Home

Entrance to the Dare Beaches by way of the Wright Memorial Bridge that spans the clear waters of Currituck Sound from Point Harbor to the sandy shores near Kitty Hawk Village, for a distance of nearly three miles.

Gateway to the famous Outer Banks. The land that has withstood the mighty forces of nature and endured the challenge of the hands of time.

Historical sites, places of interest, or beachcombing along the surf where the blue waters of the Atlantic continue to roll, will help you capture the magic of the Dare coast.

Dare County, where Virginia Dare was born, the first English child born in the New World. The land that offers many fascinating historic attractions for tourists and vacationists; where you get the true feeling of a vacation dream in reality when you stop at any of the places mentioned in the following pages; where you will be delighted with the very best that the famous Dare Beaches and historic Roanoke Island has to offer.

Your vacation does not have to be a quick checklist of every historic spot along the Outer Banks but rather an enjoyable stay where nature provides many natural resources, such as fishing, hunting, boating, surfing, swimming, and sunbathing. Savor to the soul all the essence of Dare.

POINT HARBOR RESTAURANT

Near the tall banks on the shore, at the foot of the Wright Memorial Bridge, overlooking Currituck Sound, you will find the Point Harbor Restaurant. Where you may enjoy your favorite kind of food, such as their famous Seafood Platter, sizzling choice steaks, and many others too numerous to mention, before crossing the three-million-dollar Wright Memorial Bridge to the Dare Beaches. The restaurant is open all year for your convenience.

Mr. and Mrs. Kiousis,
Owners and managers

BUCCANEER MOTEL

The Buccaneer Motel is located on U.S. No. 158 Business, in the Kitty Hawk area. An ideal place for your vacation, where you will find air-conditioned rooms, apartments and cottages, with TV and fully equipped kitchens. The ocean front, including a swimming pool, make this a wonderful playground for children.

Marian and Curtis Curling, your hosts, add much to the atmosphere that surrounds this vacation spot. Open all year round, and the climate is semi-tropical.

For reservations, write to the Buccaneer Motel; or telephone: 919-441-5133, Kitty Hawk, North Carolina.

TAN-A-RAMA APARTMENTS

Tan-A-Rama Aapartments, at Kill Devil Hills in North Carolina, are air-conditioned, have wall-to-wall carpeting, and are located at Avalon Beach near the famous Avalon Fishing Pier. Tan-A-Rama efficiencies face the cool Atlantic. Their new swimming pool makes this a perfect place for vacationing families. Conveniently located nearby are fine food stores, shops, and the pier, all are about one mile south of the Wright Brothers Memorial and Museum.

For reservations and rates, call Tan-A-Rama Apartments at Kill Devil Hills, North Carolina. Telephone: 919-441-3912.

If you desire to buy, rent, or sell real estate, contact Robert A. Young, Sr., owner and manager, at his office directly across the Highway from the Tan-A-Rama.

CROATAN INN AND LODGE

The Croatan Inn and Lodge is located at Kill Devil Hills, on the Outer Banks in North Carolina. You will love the tradition of an informal atmosphere, where good food has been served for many years. You will delight especially in their Barefoot Buffet. All on the American Plan. The air-conditioned and heated lodge, open the year round, is located on the ocean front where you will find excellent surf fishing. Kitchenettes are also available.

For reservations, call The Croatan Inn and Lodge at Kill Devil

Hills, North Carolina. Telephone—919-441-2791; R. R. Tupper, Manager.

OVRILLE WRIGHT MOTEL LODGE

For a real vacation in a quiet atmosphere, stop at the Orville Wright Motel Lodge and enjoy their spacious private beach. Also their excellent swiming pool for young and old. Here you will also find a delightful ocean-front resort Motor Hotel, with distinctive accommodations, including air conditioning, and overlooking the broad Atlantic. Located on the Dare Beaches at Kill Devil Hills, on U.S. Highway No. 158, among the ocean-front sand dunes near historic sites and the Nags Head Recreation Center along the Outer Banks of North Carolina.

OUTER BANKS TRADING POST COMPANY

Whether you are vacationing or just leisurely riding along through the famous Dare Beachs, be sure to stop at the Outer Banks Trading Post. You will find a complete line of the best in groceries at their Self-Service Market. Fresh meats and seafood daily, also garden-fresh vegetables at all times. You will delight in their charcoal-broiled hamburgers, along with your favorite drink from their Fountain Room and Luncheonette. A complete line of beer and wine, domestic and imported. Gifts, magazines, newspapers, films and cameras, are available along with their health and beauty aids.

Open to serve you every day and all year. Located on U.S. Highway No. 158 Business, near the 9-mile post, next to the Post Office at Kill Devil Hills, in North Carolina. Telephone: 919-441-5014.

MILLER'S PHARMACY, INC.

Where your health is their business. Doctor Miller is a prescription specialist, and assures his customers of the freshest and most up-to-date drugs that can be obtained anywhere in the country. Also a complete line of cosmetics, a complete soda foutnain, and toys and sunglasses are available for your convenience.

You will find Miller's Pharmacy a pleasant place ot shop for your needs. Open all year round, with cottages for rent. Located at Nags Head, a half mile south of the Carolinian, along the Outer Banks, on U.S. Highway No. 158 Business, near mile post 11. The only drugstore on the beach. Telephone: 919-441-2681, Nags Head, North Carolina.

COLONIAL INN RESTAURANT

While vacationing on the Dare Beaches, stop at the Colonial Inn Restaurant where you can enjoy a quiet delicious meal, conveniently located near the fishing pier and motel. Here your favorite food is prepared to suit your taste, whether fresh seafood, or choice steak of prime rib.

Dine in colonial atmosphere of candlelight, where service is a pleasure. Located at Nags Head, on U.S. Highway No. 158 Business, on the Outer Banks in North Carolina.

Gus Krause
Manager

THE CASINO

The playground of Nags Head Beach. Where you will find the best people from all over the world, dance to the music of such famous bands as Fats Domino, Blue Baron, Johnnie Long, Sammy Kaye, and Louis Armstrong. Where music from these famous orchestras echo around this spacious ballroom, the largest in the country. Come see the Shoe-Check Room, and the barefoot dancing. Fun and recreation for the whole family, whether it is bowling, dancing, party games, or quizo, which is played nightly. Free prizes every night.

Conventions are also held here, including ministers, sheriffs, state highway officials, Rotary, and Veterans of Foreign Wars.

The Casino is located in the heart of Old Nags Head, along the Dare Beaches, on U.S. Highway No. 158. Owned and operated by G. T. "Rass" Westcott. Telephone: 919-441-8641, Nags Head, North Carolina.

SEAFARE

The Seafare, located at Nags Head on the Dare Beaches, has well earned the good name of serving the most complete line

Wright Memorial Bridge (Connects Currituck and Dare Counties)

Wright Memorial Bridge (Connects Point Harbor and the Dare Beaches)

Point Harbor Restaurant (at the foot of Wright Memorial Bridge on the Currituck County side.)

Buccaneer Motel, Kitty Hawk, N.C. (U.S. 158 Business)

Tan-A-Rama Apartments, Kill Devil Hills, N.C. (at Avalon
Beach, on U.S. 158 Business)

Croatan Inn and Lodge, Kill Devil Hills, N.C. (U.S. 158
Business)

Orville Wright Motor Lodge, Kill Devil Hills, N.C. (U.S. 158 Business)

Miller's Pharmacy Inc., Nags Head, N.C. (U.S. 158 Business)

Colonial Inn Restaurant, Nags Head, N.C. (next to Nags Head Fishing Pier, on U.S. 158 Business)

The Famous "Casino," Nags Head, N.C. (U.S. 158 Business)

Seafare, Nags Head, N.C. (U.S. 158 Business)

Beachcomber, Nags Head, N.C. (U.S. 158 Business)

Sea Foam Motel, Nags Head, N.C. (U.S. 158 Business)

Manteo Motel Corp.

U. S. 64 and 264, Manteo, N. C. 27954

Phone 473-2101   Burwell and Ina Evans, Innkeepers

Manteo Motel Corp., Manteo, N.C. (U.S. 64 and 264)

Elizabethan Manor (new addition to the Manteo Motel Corp.),
Manteo, N.C. (U.S. 64 and 264)

of fine foods that can be found anywhere in the country. The Steak House of selections with twelve choice cuts, such as T-bone, porterhouse, top sirloin, ranging from one-and-a-quarter-thick, with excellent flavor. All are prepared on their charcoal broilers,

Any one of their sixteen varieties of Seafood Specialties will convince you, whether it is shrimp, lobster, scallops, crabmeat, or fish. North Carolina country ham steaks, Southern fried chicken, salads and desserts, are prepared to perfection.

Fifty selections of imported and domestic wines, also an international selection of beer from Germany, Holland, England, Japan, Sweden, Norway, and other countries are here for your pleasure.

Three private dining rooms for banquets and parties are available. All are air conditioned (or heated) for your comfort. Capture the flavor of Old Nags Head, dining on their chef's specialties under the spell of soft candlelight. Relax before the beautiful fireplace, and listen to the lovely sounds of real live organ melodies echoing softly around the room as you dine on your favorite dish.

The Seafare Restaurant is located at Nags Head, along the Dare Beaches on U.S. Highway No. 158 Business. Open all year. For information, inquire at the Seafare, or telephone: 919-441-5555.

THE BEACHCOMBER MOTEL

The Beachcomber Motel is located directly on the ocean front, with the carefree feeling of vacationers in the air, where cool breezes blow from the broad Atlantic. Strictly a family motel and not for groups of any kind. Rooms with or without kitchens; connecting rooms; and two-bedroom apartments. Each unit has TV and is completely air conditioned (or heated) with individual controls. All units face a beautiful swimming pool. The motel is conveniently located near fishing piers, restaurants, and shopping centers and only minutes away from the famous Fort Raleigh on Roanoke Island.

Each room with kitchen is completely furnished for housekeeping, including linens. Each room has a double bed, sofa, and a lounge chair. Others have two double beds, with tub-and-shower combination. Rollaway beds can be used when needed.

Each room without a kitchen has two double beds and rolla-ways, also bathtub and shower. Each two bedroom apartment has three double beds, or two double beds, one single, and a rollaway, and will sleep six people. Baby beds are also available. All units have daily maid service. A refrigerator is in every room. All units are reasonable rates. Open March 15, and close Thanksgiving. Surf, sound, inlet and Gulf Stream fishing can be arranged. Located a half mile North of Jennette's Fishing Pier at Nags Head, North Carolina. Telephone: 919-441-5111, or 919-441-5023.

Marvin and Hazel Minton

SEA FOAM MOTEL

Vacationing at the Sea Foam Motel is really living. It is located directly on the ocean front along the sand dunes overlooking the spacious blue Atlantic. Where you can leave your worries behind, relax on the wide clean beach, and absorb the radiant energy from the sun while cool ocean breezes blow in across the pebble-studded beach along the surf.

Here you will find thirteen efficiency apartments, thirty rooms, and two completely furnished cottages, for individual and family accommodations. All are air-conditioned (or heated). TV in every room, and individual patios. Besides two beautiful swimming pools, enjoy "Magic Fingers" shuffleboard. Up-to-date information is always available on fishing, hunting, golfing, and boating. Along with many other historic attractions, there are such as Fort Raleigh, and the Lost Colony on Roanoke Island, only minutes away. Unlimited recreation is available along the Dare Beaches nearby.

The Sea Foam Motel is located at Nags Head, North Carolina, near the 16-mile post on U.S. Highway No. 158 Business. Telephone: 919-441-3831.

THE MANTEO MOTEL CORPORATION

Stop at the Manteo Motel on historic Roanoke Island, and choose the comforts that you desire at reasonable rates. Where you will find thirty-one rooms, four efficiencies, apartments, swimming pool, room phones, TV, individually controlled heat and air conditioning, guest washer and dryer, and picnic and family recreation area. Adjoining is their beautiful restaurant with four dining rooms and excellent service. Fresh seafood comes from local waters.

The Elizabethan Restaurant at the Manteo Motel, one of the finest in the area, is open daily from 5:30 A.M. to 9 P.M. There are luncheon specials, desserts, garden-fresh vegetables, fried chicken, oysters, shrimp, fish, and crab cakes. All are delicious. Tempting Outer Banks recipes, clam chowder, and choice steaks fit for a queen. Enjoy the friendly atmosphere in the lobby where cards, stamps, and mail service are available, along with newspapers, magazines, cigarettes, sundries, souvenirs, and Lost Colony tickets and tourist information.

Stroll down the winding path through the recreation area; pitch horseshoes, play croquet, stretch out in a hammock and listen to the wind whispering through the pines, or sit on the benches and admire the lovely azalea beds.

Elizabethan Manor, a new addition to the Manteo Motel Corporation, proudly presents its twentieth century concept of sixteenth century innkeeping with richly furnished luburious rooms. Capture the magic of Old World charm—having the characteristics of the time when Elizabeth I was Queen of England—in tribute to Sir Walter Raleigh's colony.

Located on historic Roanoke Island, only three miles from the Lost Colony, on U.S. Highway No. 64 and 264, Manteo, North Carolina. Open all year. Telephone: 919-473-2101.

Burwell and Ina Evans,
Innkeepers

Many books, articles, and plays have been written about Virginia Dare, Roanoke Island, and the Outer Banks area, where the hands of time have so far failed to unravel many of the mysteries and unsolved murders, the latest being that of the beautiful Brenda Holland, a member in the cast of Paul Green's thrilling drama, *The Lost Colony*, which is produced on Roanoke Island every summer.

Plan now to take your next vacation at the Dare Beaches and capture the magic of this mystic seacoast area where you can visit many historic sites, such as the *Hattie Creef*, the Wright Brother Memorial, their living quarters and hangar, and the Cape

Hatteras Lighthouse, the tallest on the Atlantic Coast, also Bodie Island Light, both of which were destroyed during the Civil War in 1862 but were replaced in 1870-1871.

On Roanoke Island, only minutes away from the Dare Beaches, you will find Fort Raleigh National Historic site where the original fort stood back in 1585, where the English made their first attempt to settle in America. The Elizabethan gardens, resembling a sixteenth century English Garden, next to Fort Raleigh, contain many valuable statues and ornaments.

At Fort Raleigh, the *Lost Colony* drama is performed at the Waterside Theater. You can watch the last scene in the play that shows the colonists marching out of the fort into the wilderness, and get the true feeling of a country's heartbeat. It will be a keepsake in your memory.